MONSTER CINEMA

QUICK TAKES: MOVIES AND POPULAR CULTURE

Quick Takes: Movies and Popular Culture is a series offering succinct overviews and high-quality writing on cutting-edge themes and issues in film studies. Authors offer both fresh perspectives on new areas of inquiry and original takes on established topics.

SERIES EDITORS:

Gwendolyn Audrey Foster is Willa Cather Professor of English and teaches film studies in the Department of English at the University of Nebraska, Lincoln.

Wheeler Winston Dixon is the James Ryan Endowed Professor of Film Studies and professor of English at the University of Nebraska, Lincoln.

Blair Davis, *Comic Book Movies*
Steven Gerrard, *The Modern British Horror Film*
Barry Keith Grant, *Monster Cinema*
Daniel Herbert, *Film Remakes and Franchises*
Ian Olney, *Zombie Cinema*
Valérie K. Orlando, *New African Cinema*
Steven Shaviro, *Digital Music Videos*
David Sterritt, *Rock 'n' Roll Movies*
John Wills, *Disney Culture*

Monster Cinema

Cinema

BARRY KEITH GRANT

RUTGERS UNIVERSITY PRESS

New Brunswick, Camden, and Newark, New Jersey, and London

Library of Congress Cataloging-in-Publication Data
Names: Grant, Barry Keith, 1947– author.
Title: Monster cinema / Barry Keith Grant.
Description: New Brunswick : Rutgers University Press, [2018] |
Series: Quick takes: movies and popular culture |
Includes bibliographical references and index.
Identifiers: LCCN 2017053036 (print) | LCCN 2017053532 (ebook) |
ISBN 9780813588810 (E-pub) | ISBN 9780813588827 (Web PDF) |
ISBN 9780813597652 (hardback) | ISBN 9780813588803 (paperback)
Subjects: LCSH: Monsters in motion pictures. |
BISAC: PERFORMING ARTS / Film & Video /
Direction & Production.
Classification: LCC PN1995.9.M6 (ebook) |
LCC PN1995.9.M6 G69 2018 (print) |
DDC 791.43/67—dc23
LC record available at https://lccn.loc.gov/2017053036

A British Cataloging-in-Publication record for this book is
available from the British Library.

∞ The paper used in this publication meets the requirements
of the American National Standard for Information Sciences—
Permanence of Paper for Printed Library Materials,
ANSI Z39.48-1992.

www.rutgersuniversitypress.org

Manufactured in the United States of America

CONTENTS

MONSTER CINEMA

1

MEETING MOVIE MONSTERS

In the 1956 science fiction film *Them!*, when the avuncular entomologist Dr. Medford (Edmund Gwenn) sees the footprint of a giant mutated ant and realizes for the first time the insects' possible size, and the consequent threat they pose to humanity, he cries, "This is monstrous!" His words are especially apposite, for monsters, despite their seemingly unending variety, are always marked as different and, consequently, as a threat to the natural or ideological order. Movie monsters may be animal (*King Kong* [1933], *Jaws* [1975]), vegetable (*Invasion of the Body Snatchers* [1956], *Attack of the Killer Tomatoes!* [1978]), or mineral (*The Magnetic Monster* [1953], *The Monolith Monsters* [1957]). They may be human (*Psycho* [1960], *American Psycho* [2000]), inhuman (*Alien* [1979], *Life* [2017]), or technological (*Demon Seed* [1977], *The Terminator* [1984]). They may be uncomfortably small, like the turd-shaped parasites of David Cronenberg's *Shivers* (1975), or giant, like the rampaging *Amazing Colossal Man* (1957).

Indeed, the variety of movie monsters is as staggering as their appearance often is (or at least intended to
be). Some of these monsters themselves have multiple
forms. The creatures of *Alien* and its sequels and *John
Carpenter's The Thing* (1982) are capable of metamorphosis, while the vengeful wraith of *It Follows* (2014) has
the ability to take any human form. *The Blob* (1958), the
yogurt-like menace of Wes Craven's *The Stuff* (1985),
and the viscous green evil liquid of *Prince of Darkness*
(1987) are amorphous, lacking any consistent shape.
But whatever they look like, their typically repellent and
hideous physicality serves as an outward index of the
social threat they represent. Typically, their monstrosity
is marked as physically different in some way—aberrant,
freakish, repulsive—although they may be monstrous in
their very physical ordinariness, as are the pod people of
Invasion of the Body Snatchers, Norman Bates in *Psycho*,
or the elite white plotters and their mind-altered victims
in *Get Out* (2017).

Betokening the importance of the monster's physical
difference, monster movies are often structured around
the gradual reveal of the creature or creatures, building
suspense and expectation in viewers until the inevitable
"money shot," a dramatic peak when the monster in all
its intended hideousness is fully shown. In *It: The Terror from Beyond Space* (1958), for example, we first see

the creature—a Martian beast with scaly skin, ridges of teeth, and hands with three claws that sucks humans dry of all bodily fluids—as a shadow when it stows away on the ship and then in close-ups showing its horny feet or hands, and only later is its face finally revealed at a suitable dramatic moment; similarly, we see only the scaly arm and clawed hand of the eponymous gill man of *Creature from the Black Lagoon* (1954) reaching from the water's edge several times before we finally see his full body swimming underwater.

Monsters existed long before the movies, of course, rampaging through folk tales, myth, literature, and the other arts of cultures throughout the world. The foundational works of Western literature are replete with monsters: the Sirens and Polyphemus the cyclops of Homer, Virgil's harpies, Grendel of the Beowulf saga. Popular culture is populated with demons and devils, ghosts, ghouls, and golems, witches and werewolves, and, of course, zombies, the monster that has most captured the zeitgeist of the millennium. Many monsters have had sufficient appeal to generate transmedia franchises or to appear in movies because of already-established pop cult franchises, including merchandising such as comics, toys, video games, and clothing. In the 1960s, for example, the classic monsters of Universal Studios were marketed as plastic model kits by the Aurora Plastics Corporation.

The release of the studio's horror catalogue for television in the form of two "Shock Theater" packages a few years earlier helped create a young target demographic for the model kits through locally broadcast horror-film shows with colorful horror hosts like Vampira (Maila Nurmi) in Los Angeles and John Zacherle ("the cool ghoul") in Philadelphia. Zacherle also tapped into the pop-music charts with the novelty hit "Dinner with Drac" in 1958, while Vampira in turn appeared as a movie monster in Edward D. Wood Jr.'s *Plan 9 from Outer Space* (1959).

Popular music has enjoyed consistent crossovers with monster culture, from Fats Waller's "Abercrombie Had a Zombie" in 1940 to Rob Zombie, who straddles careers as musician and horror filmmaker. "The Monster Mash" was a top-ten hit (twice!) in 1962 for the Crypt Kicker Five featuring Bobby "Boris" Pickett, so named because of his ability to imitate the distinctive voice of iconic horror actor Boris Karloff. The entangled connections between the movies and popular music are insightfully satirized in Brian De Palma's *Phantom of the Paradise* (1974), a rock 'n' roll musical-horror hybrid. In short, the presence of monsters is pervasive in popular culture, from monster truck rallies to serial-killer television series to their domestication for children in the form of breakfast-cereal icons (Frankenberry, Count Chocula) and muppets that promote mathematical skills in preschoolers.

For David J. Skal, Diane Arbus's (in)famous photo-graphs of odd-looking people revealed that "'monsters' were everywhere, that the whole of modern life could be viewed as a tawdry sideshow, driven by dreams and ter-rors of alienation, mutilation, actual death and its every-day variations. . . . America, it seemed, was nothing but a monster show" (18). Many horror films suggest that their monsters represent nothing less than the corruption or fall of the United States itself. In 1960, *Psycho*, one of the first horror films to locate the monstrous within seem-ingly normal society rather than project it afar, showed that the horrors perpetrated by its youthful serial killer is less a special case than representative of a collective American disposition toward violence—a theme made explicit in Norman's comment to Marion Crane that "we all go a little mad sometimes."

George Romero's *Night of the Living Dead* (1968), another defining work of the modern American hor-ror film, begins with shots of a car on a forlorn country road, the trees bare of leaves, the low contrast of the black-and-white images further suggesting dreariness and doom. Tellingly, a roadside sign is pockmarked with bullet holes. The car then pulls into a cemetery, tomb-stones and an American flag marking the deathly land-scape. The film's negative view of the current state of the nation is continued later, in the scene on the farmhouse television showing an interviewer (played by director Romero himself) vainly trying to get answers about the crisis from officials in Washington—a scene described by one writer as seeming "to be left over from a Marx Brothers movie" (Dillard 80). A few years later, in *The Omen* (1976), an American diplomat, Robert Thorn (Gregory Peck), and his wife, Katherine (Lee Remick), adopt a child of obscure origin who seems to be an incarnation of the Devil. In the climax the Thorns are both killed, and the film concludes by showing that the Devil child Damien (Harvey Spencer Stephens) has now been adopted by the First Family, suggesting that evil has permeated to the highest levels of power and that the nation is irredeemably corrupt.

The marked presence of monsters in popular culture is addressed in a number of monster movies. In *The Stuff*, Larry Cohen's broad horror satire about junk food, we see the television ads being made and broadcast as part of the marketing campaign that succeeds in spreading the Stuff, a dangerously addictive dessert that causes internal physical changes in consumers. In *Pacific Rim* (2013), set slightly in the future when humans have been battling giant monsters for almost a decade, there are insert shots of monster action figures and video games. The absorption of "monster" rhetoric into politics and daily life is one of the themes of Gareth Edwards's *Monsters* (2010). The film posits that several years earlier, a space probe brought back an alien life form when it crashed on Earth. The alien creatures have flourished in the Central American area where it came down, now a place of regulated travel known as the Infected Zone. Photographer Andrew Kaulder (Scoot McNairy) is assigned to escort his publisher's daughter, Sam Wynden (Whitney Able), home safely by traveling through the Infected Zone. As Kaulder and Sam get close to the area, they see images of the aliens cropping up in children's drawings and on television cartoons. Road signage has come up with shorthand iconography for warning motorists about areas where aliens are frequently seen, like caution signs for animal crossings. Amid the husks of buildings destroyed by the monsters, the traditional economy has been ravaged, and a complex underground economy has arisen built around transporting people through the Infected Zone. Kaulder and Sam travel past children playing in places that are marked by destroyed military equipment or the giant carcasses of dead monsters, such otherwise disturbing intrusions apparently integrated as the new normal for the younger generation.

MONSTERS, INC.

Monsters have such a strong presence in movies that we have a name for films with them: "creature features."

Indeed, the cinema has been obsessed with monsters from the beginning. The first public film screening took place in 1895, and by 1903, pioneer French filmmaker Georges Méliès already had made numerous films with monsters, ghosts, devils, and other assorted spirits. In 1897, the same year as the publication of Bram Stoker's *Dracula*, Méliès produced, among others, *Le manoir du Diable* (*The Haunted Castle*), which featured Satan and a number of other creatures. Monsters have populated the movies ever since, all of them gestating in both timeless cultural taboos and the cultural fears of the moment.

Like all genre films, monster movies are modern society's equivalent of cultural myths. Zhang Yimou's *The Great Wall* (2016) posits an attack every sixty years by a breed of monsters called the Taotie, and a special secret division of the Imperial Army of the Song Dynasty, the Nameless Order, devoted exclusively to repelling the monsters from breaching the Great Wall of China. The movie combines historical fact with sheer fantasy for the clear purpose of creating a cultural myth. Traditionally, the term "myth" refers to a society's shared stories, usually involving gods and heroes, which explain the nature of the universe and the relation of the individual to it. In Western culture, myths, initially transmitted orally, then in print, and now in digital forms, have been disseminated by mass culture since the Industrial Revolution. Genre films, with their repetitions and variations of a few basic plots, are prime instances of mass-mediated contemporary myth. As film scholar Thomas Sobchack has written, "The Greeks knew the stories of the gods and the Trojan War in the same way we know about hoodlums and gangsters and G-men and the taming of the frontier and the never-ceasing struggle of the light of reason and the cross with the powers of darkness, not through first-hand experience but through the media" (122). Stories of monsters are timeless, no doubt beginning around the prehistoric campfire, just as John Houseman dramatically recounts the monster legend of Antonio Bay to the engrossed children in the opening scene of Carpenter's *The Fog* (1980). In mass-mediated society, we huddle around movie, television, computer screens, digital tablets, and smart phones instead of campfires for our mythic tales.

Both M. Night Shyamalan's *The Village* (2004) and Joss Whedon's *The Cabin in the Woods* (2012) are about the importance of monster myths to our culture. *The Village* is set in a community living in an isolated wilderness. The time seems to be vaguely mid-nineteenth century—there is no electricity, and the people apparently live by the fruits of their own labor—although the actual time period, which is in fact contemporary, is not clarified until late in the film. There is no trade or contact with neighboring villages, and the village elders tell stories of unseen monsters that dwell on the perimeter of their town waiting to victimize anyone who might stray into the forest, which the young are not permitted to enter. The people have constructed barriers from which they keep constant watch for these monsters.

Eventually we learn that the community exists not in the past but today, in a private tract of land in rural Pennsylvania, and that the legends of the monster have been created by the community's founders as a deliberate attempt to keep people together and the community cohesive, separate from the corrupting ways of modern technological existence. The monsters provide the community with its boundaries and limits; they are part of what shapes and defines it. The film examines how important myths of monsters are for generating and preserving communal life. Just as the existence of Frankenstein's monster galvanizes the community to come together (albeit as a cross between a search party and a lynch mob), so monsters, even as they threaten mayhem, offer the possibility of abetting social order. As Stephen King notes in his book about horror, *Danse Macabre*, "We love and need the concept of monstrosity because it is a reaffirmation of the order we all crave as human beings" (50).

In *The Cabin in the Woods*, five college students—the jock Curt (Chris Hemsworth), the scholarly Holden

(Jesse Williams), the stoner Marty (Fran Kranz), the sexually active girl Jules (Anna Hutchison), and the virginal Dana (Kristen Connolly)—gather together and head off for a weekend at a remote cabin owned by one of Curt's relatives. Their story initially unfolds like a conventional teen slasher pic: the group finds a number of strange objects, including the diary of an abused girl who had lived there in the past, and they unknowingly unleash the girl's zombified, murderous family, who proceed to attack them. This narrative is intercut with scenes of an underground technical facility where workers are preparing for and managing an important ritual. Gradually the two stories come together as we learn that the workers are entrusted with manipulating events so that conventional actions take place, that analogous rituals in other countries have failed, and that the success of the American ritual alone is the last hope for humanity to appease the ancient gods who require it. But when it seems as if the ritual will be successful, with all five stereotypical student characters being killed, Marty and Dana manage to escape into the facility, where they find and release a storehouse of various monsters, including (many of them are obligingly listed on the board in the lab) zombies, werewolves, witches, wraiths, mutants, a killer unicorn, a giant snake, a merman, and an angry molesting tree, all of which proceed to gruesomely kill everyone there.

Fleeing the slaughter, Marty and Dana come upon The Director (Sigourney Weaver), who explains to them, and to us, that such worldwide rituals are held annually to appease the Ancient Ones, a race of giant beings, in the manner of H. P. Lovecraft, who preceded the human race and who dwell underground, remaining dormant as long as the annual blood ritual is performed. The American version of the ritual requires the killing of five young people embodying certain familiar archetypes of the slasher film. It does not matter in which order the five die, as long as "the Whore" dies first. The rules are flexible regarding the Virgin's death, and there is the possibility that she can survive. But Dana cannot bring herself to shoot Marty, so the film ends with one of the Ancient Ones stirring below, its gigantic hand emerging through the floor. In other words, *The Cabin in the Woods* suggests, Americans have embraced horror generally, and the slasher film specifically, with all its conventions and clichés functioning on a mythic level to satisfy its audiences' primordial need for horrifying violence in the real world, which would otherwise erupt without such ritual entertainment to contain it.

The technicians in *The Cabin in the Woods* can manipulate events by releasing mind-altering drugs into the air of the cabin, thereby reducing, for example, the students' sexual inhibitions. Their techniques remind us that "the sleep of reason produces monsters"—the title of a famous etching (ca. 1799) by Spanish artist Francisco Goya. In Goya's image, a man writing or drawing at his desk has fallen asleep and is being besieged by a horde of winged creatures that seem like hybrids of several predatory animals, including owls, cats, and bats ("the creatures of the night," as Bela Lugosi's Dracula famously rhapsodizes). Because there is a cat at the feet of the sleeping figure, and the monsters seem to be emanating from the cat, the image might be interpreted to suggest that the sleeping figure represents the artist, whose imagination has the ability to transform the commonplace and domestic into the strange and frightening. As fiction writer Richard Wright has noted, "The artist must bow to the monsters of his imagination" (qtd. in Pine 198). Paradoxically, however, as in the case of Goya's very image, the artist's musings bring order to the wildest, most fearful of imaginings by giving it aesthetic shape.

Interestingly, in the original Spanish, the word *sueño* can mean either "sleep" or "dream." This linguistic ambiguity is especially relevant when thinking of Goya's etching in relation to film. Many critics have noted the similarities between dreaming and the experience of watching movies, some even suggesting that film viewing returns us to a womb-like, infantile state. In the dark, images flicker by, speaking to our inner self as well as to our collective psyche. For good reason, Hollywood, during the heyday of the studio era, was referred to as the "dream factory." This may explain why, while other genres have cycled in and out of popularity, the horror film has consistently been an important part of film history. With roots in such precinematic forms as medieval woodcuts, Grand Guignol theater, and the Gothic novel, horror made a smooth transition to film beginning with the one-reelers of Méliès. Mary Shelley's *Frankenstein* (1818) was filmed as early as 1910 by the Edison Company—and no less than eighty times since. Internet searches reveal that there are more than two hundred movies with "Frankenstein" in the name, although many actually have little to do with Shelley's original story. But like Frankenstein's creature, parts have been lifted from Shelley's narrative and reworked by other films to create a "Frankenstein" megatext that has the potential to expand in any direction. By 1927, even before the arrival of sound, audiences were familiar enough with horror conventions that they were being parodied in the first of several film adaptations of *The Cat and the Canary*, a haunted-house mystery.

MONSTER MASH-UP

Because the big budgets of contemporary science fiction films require them to reach the largest audience possible in order to recoup their cost and make a profit, the complexities of science fiction novels, when adapted to cinema, are often simplified while their "affective elements," the impact of the experience, is amplified (Ruddick 37). Typically, this means emphasizing the monster and its horrific nature. Most (but not all) horror movies have a monster in them, as do many (but, again, not all) science fiction films. Years ago, in the first important scholarly book on science fiction cinema, film theorist Vivian Sobchack astutely observed that "the Creature film sits (awkwardly, for some) between horror and SF" (47). Thus, such films as *Frankenstein* (1931) and *Invasion of the Body Snatchers* (as well as their source novels) are claimed with equal conviction—and justifiably so—by historians of both genres: both films provide science-fictional premises for the existence of their monsters, yet both also present them with the visual tropes of horror.

Monsters not only provide a bridge between horror and science fiction but also frequently provide the means for other forms of genre hybridization. So there are, for example, monster comedies (*Abbott and Costello Meet Frankenstein* [1948], *Shaun of the Dead* [2004]), monster musicals (*The Rocky Horror Picture Show* [1975]), and monster westerns (*Ravenous* [1999], *The Burrowers* [2008]). In the climax of *Curse of the Undead* (1959), a vampire gunfighter terrorizing a western town is killed by silver bullets in the shootout on Main Street, a clever blending of the conventions of the two genres. There are even monster music videos—most famously, Michael Jackson's *Thriller* (1983), featuring dancing zombies.

Psychological thrillers and crime films often present criminals as monstrously amoral, and movie gangsters have clear affinities with movie monsters. In John Huston's *Key Largo* (1948), when gangster Johnny Rocco (Edward G. Robinson) asks why he needs the drug shipment for which he is holding the inhabitants of a Florida hotel hostage when he is already rich, he promptly replies that the simple reason is because he wants more. While Rocco's response is, of course, eminently good business in that it encapsulates precisely the governing philosophy of corporations, his answer also speaks to the gangster's monstrous acquisitiveness, the extent to which his greed is driven by his unrestrained and unleashed desire, as is the case for many monsters. Gangsters and monsters alike are driven by oversized desires.

Just as movie monsters refuse to be contained within a single genre, so their monstrousness often derives from their transgression of normal boundaries. Monsters that were originally human, for instance, are often undead, neither alive nor dead; or they are *un*natural, a mutation or experiment gone awry. In *Them!*, a little girl traumatized by an attack on her camper by the giant ants that killed her family can only refer to the creatures by screaming the pronoun "them." In the opening title credit of *From Hell It Came* (1957), the word "IT" fills the left side of the screen in large print, after which "From Hell" and "Came" appear in smaller print, indicating that the unnameable creature (disappointingly, in this case, merely a slow-moving radioactive killer tree, discernibly a man in a monster suit) is more important than even the accursed place whence it originated. Because movie monsters transcend categories, they often cannot be named: hence *The Thing from Another World* (1951), *The Stuff, It: The Terror from Beyond Space,* and *It* (2017). As Donald A. Wandrei wrote in his 1930 horror tale "Something from Above," "It is not so much the things we know that terrify us as it is the things we do not know, the things that break all known laws and rules, the things that come upon us unaware and shatter the pleasant dream of our little world" (763).

Monsters by their very nature are "liminal creatures" who "defy borders" (Kearney 117). For philosopher Julia Kristeva, monsters are the embodiment of "abjection," which she defines as "that which does not respect borders, positions, rules, that which disturbs identity, system, order" (4). These borders may be ideological, but they also are often physical—the vampire and the zombie are undead; the werewolf and the gill man are part human, part animal—leading philosopher Noël Carroll to refer to monsters as "interstitial," a departure from that which is deemed conceptually normal and/or "natural" (55).

The borders threatened by monsters are also ideological, challenging in some way to the dominant moral order. Thematically, monster movies posit a conflict between values deemed as normal and those that threaten to violate normality, as represented by the monster. For film critic Robin Wood, the genre's "true subject" is "the struggle for recognition of all that our civilization *re*presses or *op*presses" ("Introduction" 10; emphasis in the original). Wood argues that movie monsters express the repressed desires and wishes within us. Wood's influential model of horror cinema, informed by Freudian theory, is built around this fundamental binary opposition of the normal and the monstrous. As he writes, "In so far as horror films are typical manifestations of our culture, the dominant designation of the monster must necessarily be evil: what is repressed (in the individual, in the culture) must always return as a threat, . . . ugly, terrible, obscene" (23). He provides a list of specific Others that have informed the horror genre, including women, the proletariat, other cultures, ethnic groups, alternative ideologies or political systems, children, and deviations from sexual norms (9–11).

Monster movies simultaneously allow us to disavow these secret or impure desires by projecting the forbidden outward as monstrous Others that must be destroyed.

This interpretation applies particularly well to movies featuring the premise of the beast within, as in werewolf films or the various versions of *Dr. Jekyll and Mr. Hyde*. According to such a reading, the monster represents a challenge to all those normative value sets that structure "civilization," such as patriarchy, heterosexuality, and monogamy, and so must be defeated by the (typically male) hero in order for him to take his proper place within society. As he does so, he successfully pairs with the inevitable female love interest, typically represented as the attractive daughter of the scientist or lovely lab assistant. Classic monster movies such as *Frankenstein, Dracula* (1931), and *Creature from the Black Lagoon* follow this narrative pattern particularly well.

MONSTROUS PLEASURES

But what of horror's seemingly perennial appeal? Horror is one of the few genres that is popularly defined in terms of its intended affect. While some genres such as the crime film, science fiction, and the western are defined by setting and narrative content, horror, along with comedy and pornography, is conceived around a particular emotional response. Linda Williams has referred to melodrama, porn, and horror as "body genres" because of the strong physical response elicited by each: tears in the case of melodrama, sexual arousal in pornography, and fear in horror ("Film Bodies"). The word "horror" itself derives, significantly, from the Latin *orur*, to describe the physical sensation of bristling, of one's hair standing on end. So important are such emotional and physiological responses to these genres that the extent to which films produce them in viewers is commonly used as a determining factor in judging how good these movies are. Just as a "good" porn film is one that succeeds in sexual stimulation, so a "good" horror movie is, for many viewers, simply one that succeeds in scaring them; a bad one, conversely, is one that does not.

But if monsters are as disturbing as numerous scholars and commentators have suggested, why have we perennially enjoyed them? As Stephen King sensibly wonders at the outset of his examination of horror, "why are people willing to pay good money to be made extremely uncomfortable?" (10).

The pleasures of being scared by a movie are complex, the experience analogous to that of an amusement-park attraction like a roller coaster or funhouse. In both cases, the event is controlled, part of a predetermined experience of fear that is in truth designed to keep one safe even as one is thrilled. Just as a baby enjoys the safe thrill of being tossed in the air only to be caught, a monster movie is, after all, "only a movie." Because monster movies provide us with vicarious but controlled thrills like that of an amusement-park ride, it is no accident that so many theme-park attractions, like Universal's Mummy ride, are monster oriented or that the narrative of *Jurassic Park* (1993) is built on the idea of a theme-park ride that fails. Yet monster movies serve many functions: among them, they exploit our fears of death and decay, either of the physical body or the body politic; they address our psychological need to come to terms with mortality and sexuality; they help us accept the natural order of things, including our inherently evil natures; they allow us to channel our own aggression and anger; and they provide lessons about the consequences of deviating from social norms.

Playing on the idea of the cathartic benefit of fear, William Castle's *The Tingler* (1959) is about an elusive lobster-like parasite that actually lives in the base of the human spine. It is summoned from dormancy when the human host is fearful and dissipates only when the person screams, venting their fright—otherwise the tingler would gather strength and fatally snap the person's spine. In the film, Dr. Warren Chapin (Vincent Price) is a scientist who clues into the existence of the tingler after wondering about the physiological sensations caused by fear, and he manages to extract one alive from a mute woman who is unable to scream just after he deliberately scares her to death. The creature eludes Chapin and escapes into an adjacent movie theater. First-run theaters featured "Percept-O," one of Castle's many marketing ploys, which involved mild electrical shocks delivered to randomly chosen seats, giving a slight tingle to the legs of some patrons during this scene (Brottman 268). In addition to being a pioneering effort of interactive media, *The Tingler* offers a clever metaphor for the therapeutic function of horror, which provides a release, a catharsis, of our collective and individual fears.

Some commentators have considered the appeal of horror from a more psychoanalytic perspective. Walter Evans has argued that horror films are particularly enjoyed by adolescent boys because in their awkwardness, they can easily empathize with the monsters, who are also social outcasts, and because monster films express in metaphoric form the physical changes involving the appearance of secondary sex characteristics with the onset of puberty. As Evans notes of the typical male adolescent, "Mysterious feelings and urges begin to develop and he finds himself strangely fascinated with disturbing new physical characteristics—emerging hair, budding breasts, and others—which, given the forbidding texture of the X-rated American mentality, he associated with mystery, darkness, secrecy, and evil" (54). The wolfman, for example, "sprouts a heavy coat of hair, can hardly be contained within his clothing, and when wholly a wolf is, of course, wholly naked" (54). Evans also points out that the wolfman's hairy palms (often featured prominently in transformation scenes) suggest the fate, foretold in folklore, of boys who masturbate (56).

Because monster movies are only movies, they allow us, as Nicholas Ruddick says, to "watch the monster trash the metropolis with that voyeuristic fascination that grips us when observing unpleasant events from a safe vantage point" (29). Susan Sontag understands this spectator dynamic in aesthetic as well as moral terms. For Sontag, monster movies provide the particular pleasure she calls "the aesthetics of destruction": "the peculiar beauties to be found in wreaking havoc" (213). If monster movies are weak on actual science, often amounting to little more than what H. G. Wells derisively called "scientific patter" (8), they nevertheless lure us with the kinesthetic delights of light, sound, and movement. When monsters destroy cities, often reducing famous landmarks to rubble, the destruction represents our own anger and frustrations toward social institutions. We like to vilify and expunge monsters, but we also to some extent identify with them. As Sontag puts it, monster movies provide "a morally acceptable fantasy where one can give outlet to cruel or at least amoral feelings" (215).

Sontag's idea of the "aesthetics of destruction" is alluded to in the still-life images (*nature morte* is the French term) featuring the mutilated victims of the mad and murderous protagonist of *Henry: Portrait of a Serial Killer* (1986), but it is perfectly illustrated in the kinetically charged genre hybrid *The Hidden* (1987). Combining elements of science fiction and crime thriller, the plot involves an alien law officer, "Lloyd Gallagher" (Kyle MacLachlan), who, in human form, is pursuing another alien, a thrill-seeking criminal who has the ability to enter other life forms and take them over. The monster is suitably abject, with viscous skin and tentacles, and its entrance into the body through the mouth evokes suitably monstrous disgust. But the alien makes humans do things that have appeal for many people, at least in fantasy. The creature likes stimulation, so it prefers loud head-banging music and fast cars. It cares nothing for social convention and has its human hosts take what it wants from others, using fatal violence if necessary. "I want that car," its middle-aged host body declares, looking at a red Ferrari returning to a dealership. The possessed man runs after the car, refuses to take no for an answer, kills the salesman and his customer, and coolly takes the keys and drives off. Smartly, the movie only gradually explains its premise, beginning in medias res as the alien is already inside an average guy who has just robbed a bank, shot people in the process, and escaped in a speeding sports car. As he is pursued by police, he seems oddly unemotional, and while viewers may puzzle over this, they cannot help but be swept up in the kinetic action of a rapidly edited high-speed car chase. Part of the pleasure for viewers of *The Hidden* is in watching these events unfold onscreen, being immersed in their spectacle.

In the climax, the rogue alien enters the body of a charismatic senator who is about to hold a press conference. The first question he is asked is whether he has decided if he will run for president, in response to which the inhuman senator impulsively says, to everyone's surprise, "I want to be president" before he is torched by Gallagher—a repressed urge no doubt most of us have held toward at least one politician at one time or another. The film becomes a string of such action set pieces prompted by the premise, or pretext, of alien control. Viewers can enjoy and disavow them at the same time, as these are the actions of an alien other. David Cronenberg said in regard to his own monster film *Shivers*, "Each of my films has a little demon in the corner that you don't see, but it's there. . . . People vicariously enjoy the scenes where guys kick down the doors and do whatever they want to do to the people who are inside. . . . It is obvious that there is a vicarious thrill involved in seeing the forbidden" (Beard and Handling 179). The alien in *The Hidden*, moving from host to host, is literally that "little demon" in us all.

More recently, *Colossal* (2016) addresses the idea of spectator identification with the monster from a different perspective in his offbeat take on the *kaiju eiga*, or giant monster, genre. *Colossal* focuses on Gloria (Anne Hathaway), an alcoholic party girl whose boyfriend (Dan Stevens) becomes fed up with her irresponsibility and kicks her out of his New York apartment. She retreats to her family's abandoned small-town home to regroup but meets her old school friend Oscar (Jason Sudeikis), who now owns a bar. At first, he seems like a terrific guy, and they begin to bond over nightly drinking sessions with his friends after the bar officially closes. Meanwhile, in South Korea, a giant monster appears periodically wreaking havoc and carnage in Seoul. As Gloria discovers by watching live coverage on cable news, the monster (in some way that is never satisfyingly explained, although it is somehow tied to a traumatic event Gloria and Oscar experienced together as children during a severe thunderstorm) is in fact her avatar, a projection of her when she enters a certain park in the town. With the realization, Gloria sobers up and becomes responsible for her life, not wanting to cause any further death and destruction. However, when Oscar, who also is projected as a giant robot, learns the truth, he uses the knowledge to blackmail Gloria to stay with him rather than return to her boyfriend by threatening further destruction on the poor

South Koreans. As the two tussle in the park, we watch them fight in Seoul on television, a rock-'em-sock-'em battle that looks like a fight between Godzilla and Megatron. *Colossal* thus plays with the idea that our own little failings may in fact have surprisingly enormous consequences for others. And it may also be seen as a self-reflexive meditation on the appeal of monster movies.

MONSTERS' BALL

One of the films that launched the German silent expressionist movement, *The Cabinet of Dr. Caligari* (1920), tells the tale of an evil mesmerist (Werner Krauss) who forces a somnambulist, Cesare (Conrad Veidt), to go forth under hypnosis and do his bidding, including kidnapping and murder. Cultural theorist Siegfried Kracauer perceived a trend in many of the German expressionist films to follow, including *Nosferatu* (1922), the first feature adaptation of Stoker's *Dracula*: looking back on these films after World War II, Kracauer saw them as both a harbinger and a cause of the rise of fascism in Germany. The frequent appearance of monstrous figures like the malevolent asylum director of *Caligari* and the vampire of *Nosferatu*, he argued, were symptomatic of the German people's turning away from political responsibility, from facing the real problems of the nation during a time of rampant inflation and social unrest, and reflected a wish to embrace a powerful *Übermensch* who promised to solve those problems. Just as the charismatic Caligari and Dracula drain their victims of their own will, so Hitler mesmerized the German people. Kracauer's analysis is premised on the idea that "films address themselves, and appeal, to the anonymous multitude. Popular films—or to be more precise, popular screen motifs—can therefore be supposed to satisfy existing mass desires" (5). Kracauer understood that monster movies, like most genre movies, are about the time and place in which they were made more than when and where their plots are set and that they reflect the values and ideology of the culture that produced them. This basic assumption informs the discussion of movie monsters to follow.

Our monsters embody fears that are both timeless, addressing universal taboos of sex and death, the unknown and the different, and also timely, responding to historically and culturally specific anxieties such as the dawning atomic age, ecological disaster, or the AIDS crisis. It follows, then, that the specific forms monsters take change over time, depending on evolving cultural contexts, and also that the same monsters are represented differently in different eras. So, for example, the plague-infested, fast-moving zombies of today are quite different from the voodoo-enchanted victims of early zombie movies like *White Zombie* (1932), *King of the Zombies* (1941), and *I Walked with a Zombie* (1943).

Given the number and kinds of monsters that have stalked the screen for more than a century now, any attempt to organize a short discussion about them is immediately faced with enormous difficulties, for our monsters are as protean as the various taxonomies that have been offered about them. Denis Gifford organized his early book on horror films, *Movie Monsters*, as a series of chapters each focused on a different creature: "the monster" (by which he means Frankenstein's creature), golem, mummy, zombie, vampire, werewolf, cat, ape, beast, brute, mutant, and (somewhat oddly) the mask. Drake Douglas took a similar approach in his book *Horror!*, offering chapters on each of the following creatures: vampire, werewolf, monster (again, Frankenstein's creature), mummy, walking dead (zombie), schizophrenic, and phantom. A little later, Roy Huss and T. J. Ross organized their anthology on the horror film into three categories according to type of horror: "Gothic Horror," "Psychological Thriller," and "Monster Terror," while in *Monsters and Mad Scientists*, Andrew Tudor identifies horror's "three major sub-genres": those "deriving their threat from science, those in which it derives from supernature, and those where its source is the psyche" (11–12). More recently, focusing on the monster as the one constant element of the genre, Bruce Kawin organizes the horror film into three "primary subgenres": "horror films about monsters, horror films about supernatural monsters, and horror films about monstrous humans" (*Horror* 47). "From there," explains Kawin, "one moves to the sub-subgenres, which identify the specific kind of monster or horror object the film is about. Thus, the supernatural monster movie may be subdivided into the vampire film, the ghost film, the zombie film and others," and so on (47).

I have borrowed from each of these writers at the level of chapter organization, with the three chapters to follow this introduction organized according to the type of monster involved—human, natural, or supernatural—and in that order. But I have deviated from these other works at the subgeneric level. For example, Kawin includes *Dr. Jekyll and Mr. Hyde* under the category "Transforming Monsters," along with the shape-shifting alien of *The Thing*, whereas in the simpler, broader approach offered here, I include the regressing doctor in the category of monstrous humans and *The Thing*, no matter how "unnatural" that "super carrot" may seem, in my broader category of natural monsters because it is posited as alien in origin, thus making it "natural" in the world of that film.

In chapter 2, I discuss several aspects and varieties of human monsters and the cultural and psychological fears that have generated them. Chapter 3 concentrates on monsters of nature ranging from the microscopic to the massive, from the earthly to the extraterrestrial. Lastly, chapter 4 discusses the menagerie of supernatural monsters such as demons, vampires, witches, and ghosts and the meanings of their manifestations. Rather than taking the somewhat-mechanical approach of discussing each different monster subgenre in turn, I have organized the chapters into several sections, each one devoted to exploring a different issue raised by that general category of movie monsters. The examples I have offered range across film history from the classic to the contemporary, and while I discuss some films from other nations, the emphasis is on U.S. cinema and culture.

Given the proliferation of monsters on our movie screens, no short book such as this could hope to discuss them all. But within the constraints of the present context, I hope to shed some light in an engaging and accessible way on these creatures that inhabit the darker spaces of our movie screens. The word "monster" comes from the Latin *monstrum*, referring to an unusual occurrence in nature. Such an occurrence was regarded as portending a disturbance of the natural order and was thus a sign, a warning. The root of *monstrum* is *monere*, which means both "to warn" and "to instruct." Monsters, in their otherness, do indeed offer warnings, telling us about the fears that haunt us in the real world. For Kawin, "a good horror film takes you down into the depths and shows you something about the landscape" ("Children" 361). Monster movies, then, are always about us, not "them." Even as we are invited to gaze on them as horrific spectacles, they also ask us to consider our self and soul.

2

HUMAN MONSTERS

In everyday speech, we call someone a monster when he or she acts in a way that we consider unspeakably evil or immoral. As Stephen Asma writes in *On Monsters: An Unnatural History of Our Worst Fears*, individuals are perceived as monstrous when there is a "breakdown of intelligibility" because their actions are so cruel that the public can no longer "relate to the emotional range involved" (10). So the feature film based on the life of Aileen Wournos, a female serial killer convicted and executed for murdering seven men, is titled *Monster* (2003), and *The Human Monster* (1939) is none other than Bela Lugosi as a sadistic and murderous insurance broker. Such heinous historical figures as Adolf Hitler are considered monsters, as was Vlad Tepes, also called Vlad the Impaler, known for "his habit of impaling his victims, men and women and sometimes children, on long sticks set into the ground. Some historians estimate that Vlad killed nearly a quarter of a million people in this way" (Wolf 31). Appropriately, he was transformed in the popular imagination into a literal monster, being the figure on whom Stoker based Dracula (McNally and Florescu). In the 1920s and '30s, the notorious serial killer Albert Fish was referred to in the news media as an "ogre," a "werewolf," the "Brooklyn vampire," and "the Boogeyman" (Heimer 78)—not uncommon language for describing mass murderers.

In *She Devil* (1957), a scientist (Albert Dekker) and doctor (Jack Kelly) use an experimental drug derived from the secretions of insects on Kyra Zelas (Mari Blanchard), a woman dying of tuberculosis. The drug not only cures Kyra but gives her enhanced "adaptive" abilities, making her physically strong, able to change her hair color at will, and able to heal her own injuries but also disturbing her hormonal levels and making her a murderous megalomaniac. When the two men discover the truth, they describe her as having "a warped soul" and admonish themselves for having created "an inhuman being." The cinema is filled with monstrous inhumans—serial killers, sadistic Nazis, mad scientists—and their victims. People have been turned into monsters through a variety of means, including electricity, atomic radiation, wonder drugs, alien takeover, and imposed surgery. In that last category, the list of human monsters in the movies who have been genetically spliced with animals is staggering: people have been turned into, among others creatures, flies, alligators, snakes, spiders, chickens, wasps, jelly-fish, walruses, and a metaphoric human centipede. As Denis Gifford notes, "Man has been metamorphosed into a whole menagerie of monstrous animals, and even vice versa" (108).

MONSTROUS BODIES

Like monsters, people with visible physical differences— "freaks," as they were called until the term was deemed politically incorrect in recent times—challenged the boundaries of the status quo, the normal. Bearded ladies, Siamese twins, JoJo the Dog-Faced Boy, and others were popular features at carnival freak shows, challenging in different ways the normal understanding of identity and humanness. (In the 1960s, hippies proudly referred to themselves as "freaks" because they thought of them-selves as being in opposition to "the Establishment.") The "monsters" most like us, freaks were forced to make a living putting themselves on display for the voyeuristic pleasure of a society that regarded them as Other while assuring itself of its normality. Physical freaks are merely biological anomalies, although decidedly human, yet they are often regarded as monstrous. This point is emphati-cally demonstrated in David Lynch's *The Elephant Man* (1980), based on the actual life of Joseph Merrick (in the film called John), a severely deformed man (his condition was never definitively diagnosed) in Victorian England. The film begins with Merrick on display in a freak show. "Rescued" from there, later he is accepted by a curious high society that once again makes him the object of a normative gaze, however unintentional. When Merrick is chased and cornered in the streets by an angry mob, he cries, "I am not an elephant! I am not an animal! I am a human being! I . . . am . . . a man!"

Movies have often espoused such liberal sentiments even as they have not always practiced what they have preached. Actor Rondo Hatton, who suffered from acromegaly, a disease of the pituitary gland that causes physical deformation, was typecast as monstrous villains like the Hoxton Creeper in *The Pearl of Death* (1944) and *House of Horrors* (1946), as well as a leper (*The Moon and Sixpence* [1942]), a hunchback (*Sleepy Lagoon* [1946]), a gorilla (*The Princess and the Pirate* [1946]), and Moloch the Brute (*The Jungle Captive* [1945]), sometimes playing without makeup. The typecasting of Hatton made visible in films the demonization as monstrous those people with anomalous bodies. With cinema, the public gaze of the camera replaced the actual freak show that preceded it.

Nowhere is this mixed message more apparent than in the infamous *Freaks* (1932), directed by Tod Browning the year after he directed *Dracula*. The film uses actual "freaks" (many of whom, such as Koo Koo and Prince Randian, were in fact real sideshow performers) in the cast. The film's story is set in a traveling circus, where the so-called freaks share a moral protocol—"the code of the freaks"—according to the carney, "a law unto themselves" for mutual protection in a hostile world. When the trapeze artist, Cleopatra (Olga Baclanova), overhears one of the midgets, Hans (Harry Earles), mention a cache of money he has saved, she hatches a plan with her lover, the strong man Hercules (Henry Victor), to marry Hans and then poison him to inherit the money. The deluded Hans marries Cleo and is immediately treated brutally by her as she begins to poison him. In the climax, the freaks discover her plot and unite to seek vengeance by killing Hercules and mutilating Cleopatra.

Early on the film emphasizes that the so-called freaks are not really very different from us: we see them doing domestic chores like hanging laundry, for example, showing how much they are "like us" and that difference is only skin deep (Hawkins 267). Two of the physically normal people, Cleopatra and Hercules, seem morally monstrous, willing to exploit and even kill for material gain, while the "freaks" seem admirably loyal by contrast. As Ivan Butler writes, "Browning has turned the popular convention of horror topsy-turvy. It is the ordinary, the apparently normal, the beautiful, which horrify—the monstrous and distorted which compel our respect, our sympathy, ultimately our affection. The visible beauty conceals the unseen evil, the visible horror is the real goodness" (Butler 65).

Yet in presenting the strangely bodied circus people as objects of our voyeuristic gaze, the film falls into the same trap it preaches against. The promotional material for the film's initial release encouraged viewers to look at them. "Unlike anything you've ever seen," proclaimed one ad for the film: "The *strange* and *startling* love-drama of a *midget*, a lovely *siren*, and a *giant*!" In addition to the film's stars, the ad highlights "a horde of caricatures of creation— not actors in make-up—but living, breathing creatures as they are and as they were born!" (Hawkins 265). The circus barker begins the opening scene by promising, "we have living, breathing monstrosities." Just as this sensational advertising copy emphatically positions the "freaks" as horrible monsters at which we may gawk, the film's climax presents them as frightening monsters. In an intense rainstorm, they slither and crawl through the mud, associating them with muck and disgust, to exact their revenge on Cleopatra. Lightning flashes alternate with disturbing darkness, allowing us to glimpse them only momentarily and starkly. The camera looks straight on as they threateningly approach it and, by extension, us. The Living Torso, lacking arms and legs, undulates with a knife in his mouth, as does one of the crawling pinheads. In short, their swarming vengeance in the scene seems to endorse the very view of the "freaks" as freaks, as monsters rather than as people. As they approach Cleopatra in the unknown darkness of the forest, the film cuts away, as if what is to follow is too horrible to witness, to the final scene, back at the circus at a later time as the carney reveals to his audience, and to us, "the most astounding living monstrosity of all time"—Cleopatra, now a chicken with a human head nestled in a bed of hay, clucking away. Thus, although the film seeks to generate sympathy for those who are physically different, it ultimately contradicts its own good intentions by associating them with the tropes of horror and positioning them as monsters.

If horrifying physical difference is not congenital in monster cinema, it is usually the result of bad science. *Man-Made Monster* (1941) straightforwardly expresses this common fear in monster movies. Lon Chaney Jr. plays "Dynamo" Dan McCormick, a good-hearted but not very bright carnival performer whose act involves administering small doses of electricity to himself. He comes to the attention of mad scientist Dr. Paul Rigas (Lionel Atwill), who exposes an unknowing Dan to increasing amounts of electricity as he cackles about turning him into a superman for the purposes of world domination. Instead, Dan becomes drained of vitality, wandering about indifferently, like a zombie, needing periodic fixes of high voltage. As Dan becomes more electrified, the unassuming nice guy of the film's first half who loved puppies and walked happily in the sun becomes monstrously indifferent and joyless in the second. Dan is at once victim and monster, the result of putting his faith in a medical science beyond his simple understanding—a fear that has only grown today with the availability of increasingly sophisticated and drastic medical interventions.

Medical invasiveness in monster movies often takes the form of monstrous metamorphosis exploiting fears regarding rape, cancerous tumors, and the very integrity of the physical self. In monster movies, these fears are often presented as forced penetration by another life form, resulting in the parasitic growth of an alien within the body, whether the progenitor is supernatural (*Rosemary's Baby* [1968]), technological (*Demon Seed*), or alien (*Village of the Damned* [1960]). The horrifying idea of monstrous parturition, where the body is at the mercy of parasitic processes beyond one's control, is expressed most powerfully in the unforgettable scene in *Alien* when Kane, awake and seemingly fine after being freed from the face-hugger, is having dinner with the rest of the crew when he begins to spasm and with a horrible screech the newborn alien bursts through his ribcage, blood and viscera spewing. In the prequel *Prometheus* (2012), inter-planetary archeologist Elizabeth Shaw (Noomi Rapace) is so horrified by the prospect of being impregnated by alien sperm that she performs an abortion on herself with an automated surgical unit.

InAlienable (2008), written by Walter Koenig (Ensign Chekov of TV's *Star Trek*) concerns an impregnated male. A scientist, Dr. Eric Norris (Richard Hatch), is given by a local acquaintance a curious object that comes to Earth along with a meteor. Unbeknownst to Norris, a tentacled creature emerges and enters his body, splicing its DNA with his in an alien fetus. The film seems to move in the direction of Cronenbergian body horror, with Norris's body swelling and changing as the alien entity grows within him; but then it unexpectedly shifts to a sobering courtroom drama for its second half after the initially horrified Norris, who suffers from past guilt regarding the deaths of his wife and child in a car accident while he was driving, embraces the creature as a son when it is "born." The creature, named "Benjamin" (Gabriel Pimentel, Bradley Laise), has a humanoid body but a disturbingly alien-looking face and six long tentacles on its back. Benjamin grows rapidly but is quickly seized by government agents, who turn it over for experimentation to Norris's lab, run by a vindictive administrator motivated by personal revenge against Norris. The creature's health deteriorates without being near Norris, who goes to court to regain custody of Benjamin.

InAlienable offers us the spectacle of bodily penetration and impregnation but then, after inviting a horrific response from viewers, asks us to reflect on that response and our underlying assumptions about how we define and distinguish us from "them," the normal from the monstrous. In the trial, which takes up the second half of the film, defense and prosecuting attorneys argue over very real legal issues such as the concept of habeas corpus and the definition of a "person" and "human being." Racial issues enter the trial when an expert's testimony involves a comparison between the amount of human DNA in Benjamin and the rights of a hypothetical octaroon. People outside the courthouse demonstrate on both sides of the argument, brandishing placards that demand protection for Benjamin and others calling him "monster," reflecting the ideological rift in the culture beyond the courtroom. When Benjamin is displayed before the court, the government's lawyer (Marina Sirtis) asks the jury rhetorically, "Would you want this thing crawling around your family?" connecting the film's legal debate to the real racial tensions in the nation and the world. Before the verdict can be delivered, a crazed observer pulls a gun and shoots Benjamin, killing him. The unresolved ending suggests that the deep racial and ethnic tensions the film addresses have yet to be resolved, even as new biotechnologies such as cloning and artificial insemination have an increasing presence in our lives.

In Kevin Smith's *Tusk* (2014), a crazed amateur scientist, Howard Howe (Michael Parks), drugs his victims and attempts to transform them into walruses through a series of surgeries. Howe's motive, as he reveals in his obligatory monologue to his new victim, smug podcaster Wallace Bryton (Justin Long), is a twisted take on the wish to return to the womb: in the past, he had been a shipwrecked sailor, and while the other men behaved brutally to each other trying to survive, he found protection and sustenance in the carcass of a walrus. While Howe's motive in *Tusk* is purely personal, most movie mad scientists suffer from more grandiose reasoning, wanting to usurp God. For Ina Rae Hark, the mad scientist "is an individual who, in a quest to unlock the secrets of nature and harness them to his will, transgresses limits self-imposed by other men and in doing so creates, unleashes, or authorizes the monstrous" (303). Dr. Jack Griffin (Claude Rains) in *The Invisible Man* (1933) is a paradigm of such scientific overreachers: at first, he plays delightedly with his invisibility, but the new drug that made him transparent quickly changes him into a megalomaniac who now aims at domination.

In *Frankenstein*, Dr. Henry Frankenstein (Colin Clive) is clearly mad because he attempts to usurp the place of God in creating life. Exulting in the success of his experiment of creating a human being, he must be restrained by his friend Victor (John Boles) and mentor, Dr. Waldman (Edward Van Sloan), as he gazes skyward and proclaims, "Oh—in the name of God. Now I know what it feels like to be God!" The lifting of the creature on his slab into the sky during a thunderstorm to give it an animating jolt of electricity is (like the bolts in the creature's neck) entirely an invention of the film and further suggests the overreaching of Frankenstein as his handiwork extends to the very heavens. Such "mad" doctors are treated as monstrous because they are shown as exceeding the "proper"—that is, the known—bounds of scientific inquiry; by usurping the role of God, they express our collective anxieties about the advances of medical science with their potential for unlocking the secrets of life and death.

These movies typically end conservatively, with the mad scientist dead, often because of the very thing he had been experimenting with, and someone musing aloud, making explicit the movie's moral that there are places humanity was not meant to go. So, for example, at the end of *Island of Lost Souls* (1932), the first of three adaptations of H. G. Wells's 1896 novel *The Island of Dr. Moreau*, after the experimental vivisectionist Moreau (Charles

Laughton) is attacked and killed by the beast-people hybrids he had created, providing a sense of poetic justice, shipwrecked protagonist Edward Parker (Richard Arlen) escapes the scientist's island compound with his fiancée, Ruth (Leila Hyams), by boat, telling her not to look back at the island as it goes up in flames.

MONSTROUS MINDS

A similar ending to *Island of Lost Souls* informs *Forbidden Planet* (1956), a monster movie in which the central character, living on another planet in the future, seeks to distinguish himself from what he refers to as "the mad scientists of the taped thrillers." In the plot, the crew of United Planets Cruiser C-57D arrives at the planet Altair IV to investigate what happened to an earlier ship of colonists that had landed there years before. Oddly, the only survivors are Dr. Morbius (Walter Pidgeon) and his beautiful daughter, Alta (Anne Francis), aided by a robot named Robby. Morbius warns Commander Adams (Leslie Nielsen) and his landing party about a mysterious unseen creature that had killed all the other colonists and may strike again. Eventually it is revealed that Morbius had boosted his intelligence with the aid of a machine built by the original inhabitants of the planet, the Krell, but that it also had provided the means for him unknowingly to project his own incestuous desires ("jealousy," as the film euphemistically puts it) outward in embodied form as "the monster from the id," which is responsible for the killings. The Krell, on the technological verge of "eliminating all instrumentalities" through the power of their thought machines, had also unleashed their own primitive instincts and so destroyed themselves virtually overnight.

John Baxter refers to the 1950s—a decade that, spurred by Cold War anxieties, the Space Race, and a rash of UFO sightings, saw a glut of monster movies beginning with *The Thing from Another World* and *The Day the Earth Stood Still* in 1951—as "Springtime for Caliban," in reference to the misshapen creature of William Shakespeare's final play, *The Tempest* (1610). Baxter's metaphor is especially relevant to *Forbidden Planet*, with its narrative that parallels that of Shakespeare's play. The story of *The Tempest* involves a magician, Prospero, living on an enchanted island with his beautiful daughter, Miranda, and their meeting with a group of shipwrecked noblemen. In *Forbidden Planet*, Prospero is transposed into Dr. Morbius, Miranda into Alta, and the shipwrecked Italian nobles of the play become the crew of the spaceship. In Shakespeare's play, Ariel is an ethereal, benevolent spirit, the agent of Prospero's magic who performs all his spells and illusions for the magician; and Caliban, the son of a witch, is a brutish, physical creature who lusts after Miranda. In the film, Ariel becomes Robbie the Robot, a machine capable not only of synthesizing whatever is needed, like lead shielding and whiskey, but of a droll wit, while "the monster from the id" is the film's version of Caliban.

According to Sigmund Freud, the id is that part of the psyche that "is filled with energy reaching it from the instincts, but it has no organization, produces no collective will, but only a striving to bring about the satisfaction of the instinctual needs subject to the observance of the pleasure principle. . . . The id, of course, knows no judgments of value; no good and no evil; no morality" (75–76). The presence of the young, attractive, miniskirted, and sexually innocent Anne Francis seems enough to release any healthy heterosexual male's repressed id, and, as we are told, the ship's all-male crew has been locked up in hyperspace for a year. In the film's climax, Commander Adams comes to understand the nature of the beast, and he provides an astonishingly concise summary of Freudian theory to Morbius: "We are all part monsters in our subconscious—that's why we have laws and religion. You sent your secret id out, a primitive, more enraged and inflamed with each frustration. You still have the mind of a primitive." Morbius realizes, along with the viewer, that the monster is in fact the embodied projection of his own incestuous desire for his daughter, smashing its way through every physical obstacle, including "solid Krell metal, twenty-six inches thick." But then, finally comprehending, Morbius renounces his own libidinous desires, and the monster evaporates as Morbius expires, his brain overloaded from the Krell machinery.

In the end, Commander Adams, the new Adam, leaves the garden with his nubile Eve. Morbius's scientific meddling has brought to light the dark urges that, according to Freudian theory, require repression for society to function. Thus, Morbius, despite his protestation to the contrary, is yet one more in a long line of mad scientists, for he has violated the prime directive of so many science fiction and horror movies, that there are places in nature where humanity was not meant to go—even when it has achieved the ability to travel the stars. The film ends conservatively, much like the endings of, for instance, *Island of Lost Souls* and, as discussed later, *Dracula*, by putting the lid back on the id. Back in the spaceship, Adams and Alta, the newly formed heterosexual couple, shield their eyes from the explosion of the planet, triggered by Krell failsafe technology, and instead look forward to returning to Earth to assume their place in normative society. It may be that, to quote Prospero's concluding words in *The Tempest*, "We are such stuff as dreams are made on," but in *Forbidden Planet*, it is also true, as the ship's doctor assesses, that "anywhere in the galaxy, this is a nightmare" from which it is good to awaken.

Morbius's name, while also invoking the Latin word *mors*, meaning "death," also alludes to the Moebius strip—a topological configuration that is a two-dimensional figure with only one surface. That is, it contains two sides in one. In other words, Dr. Morbius, like us all, is a double, two people in one: the civilized self and the primitive beast. As Harvey Greenberg writes, "We are repeatedly admonished in weird cinema that even the gentlest of men may bare fangs and bay at the moon when his passions are kindled" (199). But just as Prospero breaks his staff, buries his book of enchantments, and renounces his magic at the conclusion of Shakespeare's play, so in the film's climax, Morbius, dressed in the robe of an alchemist—and thus associating science with black magic—acknowledges his own responsibility even as, according to the logic of Hollywood morality, he must die for the sin.

Morbius's two sides, the rational scientist and the monstrous id, constitute a variation of the double, a central trope of classic monster stories such as Edgar Allan Poe's "William Wilson" (1839) and Robert Louis Stevenson's *Strange Case of Dr. Jekyll and Mr. Hyde* (1886) as well as of most movie werewolves. Many of the cinema's human monsters look normal physically but are monstrous on the inside, their mental monstrousness often projected outward as a literal or figurative double. For Robin Wood, the double motif is "the privileged form" of "the return of the repressed" (the monster) in the horror genre ("Gods and Monsters" 21). But while movie monsters are often positioned as the external projection of a character's repressed desires, *Forbidden Planet* is unique in that it labels its invisible monster explicitly as deriving from subconscious desires according to psychoanalytic theory.

MOTHER OF ALL MONSTERS

Alfred Hitchcock's *Psycho* (1960), based in part on notorious real-life serial killer Ed Gein (as was Leatherface in *The Texas Chainsaw Massacre* [1974] and Buffalo Bill in *The Silence of the Lambs* [1991]), is a film built around a variation of the double motif. The story involves a schizophrenic motel operator named Norman Bates (Anthony Perkins), whose personality has been partially taken over by that of his long-dead domineering mother; a secretary in a real-estate office, Marion Crane (Janet Leigh), who steals $40,000 from her employer in order to marry her indebted fiancé, Sam Loomis; and their random, fateful meeting. Driving with the stolen money to rendezvous with the unsuspecting Sam, Marion spends the night at Bates's quiet motel off the main highway, where she arouses Norman's sexual desire, resulting in his vengeful and jealous "mother" killing Marion in a guilty rage. After Arbogast (Martin Balsam), a dogged private detective hired by Marion's employer, also disappears while on her trail at a local motel, Sam and Marion's sister, Lila (Vera Miles), check into the motel posing as motorists. After a struggle with Norman in which he is subdued, the truth is learned by the characters and the audience: Norman had killed his mother and her lover years ago, had stolen and preserved her corpse, and had given over part of his personality to her in order to create the illusion that she was still alive and to manage his matricidal guilt.

Both main characters are doubled. Marion is a respectable career woman who is also a thief, while Norman is a pleasant young fellow who is also a psychotic serial killer: both have secret selves at odds with their respectable exteriors. The plot, too, is split, with the first part following Marion and the second part Norman. Doubles also appear frequently in the images, with Marion doubled several times by her reflection in mirrors and an emphasis on the visual resemblance between actors Anthony Perkins and John Gavin in profile when they talk in the motel office. When Norman invites Marion to dinner, they are on opposite sides of the frame, with Marion doubled by her reflection in a dresser mirror; and when he brings the tray of food to her, their positions are reversed in the frame, and it is now Norman who is reflected in one of the motel windows.

Norman's observation about the universal potential for monstrous madness—"We all go a little mad sometimes"—gives voice to Hitchcock's view of the duality of human nature, a theme he consistently explored in his films. But in *Psycho*, Hitchcock takes the idea further by luring viewers into this dynamic through the processes of identification, so that the film's vision of the monstrous is not only the psychopathic character Norman Bates alluded to in the film's title or the impulsive secretary Marion but also everyone in the audience (Wood, *Hitchcock's* 142–49). As viewers trained by Hollywood, we are inevitably disturbed when we watch *Psycho* and see our apparent protagonist, Marion, suddenly and brutally killed, eliminated from the narrative after we have been encouraged so intensely by Hitchcock to identify with her through such techniques as the frequent use of close-ups of Marion's face, for example, and the privileging of her unspoken thoughts in voice-over as she imagines what will happen in the office on Monday when she and the money are discovered missing. As Marion is followed for a time by the faceless and vaguely disquieting state trooper, the "Cop of the Mind," viewers are "seduced into applauding the theft, surrendering our scruples and assenting to Marion's criminality" (Greenberg 118,

117) because we come to root for her and for her wish for respectability and marriage. Marion even decides to redeem herself morally by deciding to return the money she stole. And then she showers, cleansing herself of her guilt, making us even more comfortable identifying with her just before she is killed.

As Robin Wood suggests, when Marion is killed, viewers have no choice but to transfer their identification to Norman. This transference is literalized in the movement of the camera, as it pulls back and away from Marion's dead, unblinking eye to Norman's horrified response at the discovery of her body in the bathroom. And then we watch a good son's protective cleanup after his mother's mess ("a boy's best friend is his mother," he had told Marion earlier) in a scene that Hitchcock extends well beyond the time required to advance the plot. The film ends with an interior monologue of "Mother," who has now repressed Norman's consciousness completely, thinking to show everyone how harmless "she" is by not swatting the fly on her hand as "she" returns the gaze of the camera. Earlier we had looked through the office peephole, along with Norman, at Marion undressing for her shower; now, at the end, when Norman looks back at the spectator, we are forced to confront our own moral culpability.

In the American cinema of the postwar era, the monsters began coming home to roost. The same cultural and social anxieties that emerged in the downbeat genre of film noir subsequently found their way into monster cinema. *Psycho*, along with *Invasion of the Body Snatchers* in 1956, was a pivotal monster film in that it situated its monster so emphatically within the normal and the commonplace rather than elsewhere. *I Walked with a Zombie* is set in a West Indian jungle; *Island of Lost Souls* is set on an uncharted island in the Pacific. *Dracula* take place in a Transylvania of the imagination; crossing the Borgo Pass represents a crossing of a distinct threshold from the rational world into a world of nightmares. Such different and mysterious locales allowed for the development of expressionist atmosphere, of course, but also suggested American culture's collective disavowal of the monster from the id and its consequent projection onto others.

By contrast, the locations of *Body Snatchers* include a nondescript doctor's office, a suburban patio, and the middle-American town square, and *Psycho*'s settings are equally mundane: among them, a real-estate office, a used-car lot, and a motel (including a bathroom with toilet!). In the opening shots of *Psycho*, the camera moves from the airy openness of a sunny afternoon to the dark, enclosed interior of a hotel room, first picking out one of many windows, the blind partially drawn for privacy. The occupants clearly have something to hide, but as the camera looks into the room, the lens aperture opens, letting more light in and showing us what is hidden within. This opening functions as a microcosm of the movement of the film as a whole, from nondescript normality to the heart of darkness it covers.

Psycho, presaging a decade that seemed filled with monstrous mass murderers and serial killers, from Charles Whitman to Charles Manson, certainly was not the first serial-killer film to ascribe the killer's murderous compulsion to psycho-sexual dysfunction rooted in the familial past. Such movies as *The Lodger* (1944), a Jack the Ripper tale, Fritz Lang's *While the City Sleeps* (1956), and Hitchcock's own *Shadow of a Doubt* (1943), among others, preceded it. But these earlier films tended to employ the conventions of film noir and crime thrillers, whereas *Psycho* works squarely in the tradition of horror ("this was a crime of passion, not profit," explains the psychiatrist at the end) with its old, dark house behind the clean motel (the space suggestive of the mind's interior, the ego "in front" of the dark id "behind"), the two shocking murders, the basement, and Bernard Herrmann's violins playing pizzicato on the soundtrack.

MONSTROUS SEX

Serial killers are often depicted in movies as monsters, like "Hannibal the Cannibal" Lector (Anthony Hopkins) in *The Silence of the Lambs*, who wears a muzzle and is so frightening that he is kept in top-security isolation. *Psycho* not only inspired several imitations, including a cycle of similar psycho-sexual horror movies such as William Castle's *Homicidal* (1962), but might also be seen as a progenitor of the slasher film, which began with *Halloween* (1978). Carpenter's *Halloween* in turn spawned a cycle of slasher films in which, typically, psychotic males set about systematically killing an isolated group of people, usually female teenagers. Often the killer is motivated by a past trauma activated by the promiscuity of the victims he stalks, and the killings often seem to be a punishment for being sexually active or precocious. The famous opening tracking shot of *Halloween* is from young Michael Myers's point of view as he comes into the house and discovers his sister having sex with her boyfriend, a primal scene that seems to trigger his murderous spree. This convention is employed in such slashers as *Friday the 13th* (1980), *A Nightmare on Elm Street* (1984), and their numerous sequels—leaving limited room for variation, as explained in *The Cabin in the Woods*. In *The Final Girls* (2015), its title referring to Carol Clover's influential examination of gender in the slasher film, the daughter of a former slasher scream queen finds herself thrust into the world of her mother's big hit, "Camp Bloodbath," where she must follow the conventions along with the stereotyped fictional characters there in order to survive.

Often coded as supernatural monsters, these serial killers sometimes seem immortal, to return from seemingly fatal injuries again and again, like a persistent nightmare. In *Halloween*, Michael Myers's psychiatrist, Dr. Sam Loomis (his name a reference to Marion's boyfriend in *Psycho*), describes his patient as evil incarnate, the "bogeyman." The convention of costuming the killer in a mask of some kind—Leatherface's skin mask in *The Texas Chainsaw Massacre*, Michael's disturbingly featureless mask in *Halloween*, Jason's hockey mask in *Friday the 13th*, Ghostface's "Scream" mask in *Scream* (1996)—emphasizes his monstrous otherness, for it distances us from him, preventing significant identification with him. As Vera Dika observes, in wearing a mask, the slasher is "depersonalized," "the more intricate workings of his consciousness hidden" (88). He is at once anybody and nobody, like the nondescript guy in George Romero's *Bruiser* (2000) who is unable to remove a blank mask from his face. For Bruce Kawin, the mask gives slashers "a mythological edge, as if they have become pure forces of anonymous destruction, figures out of their own myths" (142).

According to Wood, the slasher and "teeny-kill pic" "represent a sinister and disturbing inversion of the significance of the traditional horror film: there the monster was in general a 'creature from the id,' not merely a product of repression but a protest against it, whereas in the current [slasher] cycle the monster . . . has become essentially a superego figure, avenging itself on liberated female sexuality or the sexual freedom of the young" ("Beauty" 63). The slasher films evolved into the subgenre of the erotic thriller, in which sexual transgression, even between consenting adults, inevitably turns deadly. The cycle was launched by the box-office success of *Fatal Attraction* (1987), with its plot involving a one-night stand between a married family man, Dan Gallagher (Michael Douglas), and a professional woman, Alex Forrest (Glenn Close), who then becomes increasingly psychotic and possessive, ultimately trying to kill Dan and his family. Like the serial slashers, Alex is coded as a monster in the climax: she invades the family home on a murderous rampage and seems almost supernaturally unstoppable, like Jason Vorhees and Michael Myers. When Alex is apparently drowned in the bathtub by Dan, after an improbably lengthy period of time, she bursts from the tub and then must be killed again, shot by Dan's wife, Beth (Anne Archer).

Erotic thrillers such as *Fatal Attraction*, *Basic Instinct* (1992), and *Indecent Proposal* (1993) depicted anxiety, confusion, and distrust over changing sexual attitudes as society moved toward the millennium, particularly the institutionalization of harassment guidelines in the workplace and the anxieties over AIDS and other STDs—the latter a fear that also fueled other monster movies such as David Cronenberg's remake of *The Fly* (1986), which chronicles the horrific spectacle of Seth Brundle's atrophying human body (he collects the parts in his bathroom medicine cabinet as they fall off). Defined by Linda Ruth Williams as "noirish stories of sexual intrigue incorporating some form of criminality or duplicity, often as the flimsy framework for on-screen softcore sex" (1), the erotic thriller in turn has been supplanted by the more explicit films of the New Extremism, especially a cycle of films from France that includes Catherine Breillat's *À ma soeur* (*Fat Girl*, 2001), Gaspar Noé's *Irreversible* (2002), and Bruno Dumont's *Twentynine Palms* (2003). These films and others of the cycle employ conventions of horror and monster cinema in the intensely politicized context of contemporary gender and sexual relations.

Breillat's *Fat Girl* involves two teenage sisters, one, Elena Pingot (Roxane Mesquida), conventionally beautiful, the other, Anaïs (Anaïs Reboux), overweight and dumpy. In the film's lengthy and controversial set piece, during a summer vacation, Elena has anal sex in the girls' shared bedroom with a smooth-talking boy, while her sister, turned away in her bed, cannot help but overhear what is going on as she pretends to be asleep. When their mother (Arsinée Khanjian) discovers what has happened, she abruptly ends the holiday and hustles her daughters into the car to drive back home. As night approaches, they pull over to a highway rest stop to doze. When Elena and her mother fall asleep, Anaïs stares off into the distance. And then this moment of quiet is suddenly shattered along with the car's windshield as a man breaks it with a hammer, which he also slams into Elena's head, killing her instantly, after which he strangles the mother. He then pursues Anaïs into the adjacent woods, followed by a fade to the final scene, in which police are investigating the vehicle and leading a dazed Anaïs out of the woods as she claims that she was not raped. Whether the violent attack really happened or represents the monstrous return of the repressed for Anaïs, who throughout has expressed her disgust with men and resentment toward her sister, is ultimately unclear. Either way, the shattered windshield represents an attempt by Breillat to push our fear of the monstrous beyond the barrier of the cinema screen in a way analogous to Hitchcock's rending of the shower curtain in *Psycho*.

Like *Fat Girl*, *Irreversible*, and *Twentynine Palms*, Alexandre Aja's *High Tension* (*Haute Tension*, 2003) views patriarchal masculinity as monstrous. The plot borrows from both the slasher film and the home-invasion horror film. Marie (Cécile de France) goes with her college friend Alex (Maïwenn Le Besco) to the latter's family home in the country for a quiet study weekend. But the house is invaded by a murderous middle-aged man who proceeds to kill the entire family, except for Alex, whom he imprisons in his van, where Marie hides and tries to free her as he drives away. The killer stops at a gas station, and before Marie can warn the attendant, the murderer kills the attendant with an axe. The killer leaves, and Marie follows him in the attendant's car. When the police arrive to investigate, they look at the video surveillance footage for clues, and along with them, we see that it was actually Marie who axed the attendant. We suddenly realize, only fifteen minutes before the film's end, that Marie is in fact a psychopathic killer with a split personality who imagines herself as a male killer. When the film cuts back to Marie, who has seemingly vanquished the killer and is now "rescuing" Alex from the back of the van, we come to understand that Marie has desired Alex—she was "touched by her, aroused by her," as the psychiatrist says about Norman Bates after he spied on Marion in the shower—and that, like Norman, she is so riddled with repressed guilt that she has failed to acknowledge her own feelings. Once Marie frees Alex in the van, Alex escapes, pursued by Marie brandishing a concrete saw, a gendered inversion of Leatherface in *The Texas Chainsaw Massacre*. As Marie declares that she will never let anyone come between them, Alex impales her through the shoulder with a crowbar she had taken from the car's toolbox.

In retrospect, the reason for Marie's madness is attributable to the cultural pressures of heterosexuality, a point established early in the film as the two women chat about relationships and dating. Alex asks Marie when she is going to take "the plunge," assuming the inevitability and universality of heterosexuality. Marie deflects the question by asserting, "I'm not sex mad"—which, of course, as we find out, is precisely what she is because her "forbidden" desire has been pathologized by normal society. But that "cauldron of seething excitations," as Freud called the id (73), quickly boils over once her desire is triggered by seeing Alex showering. Linda Williams writes that "the power and potency of the monster body in many classic horror films . . . should not be interpreted as an eruption of the normally repressed animal sexuality of the civilized male (monster as double for male) but the feared power and potency of a different kind of sexuality (the monster as double for woman)" ("When" 22). Marie represses her "perverse" desire, disavowing it by recasting it in the vilest, most aggressive masculine form she can imagine. Visually, the killer represents a generalized working-class "maleness," like the psychotic working-class killers in *In Cold Blood* (1967), *The Texas Chainsaw Massacre*, and *Wolf Creek*

(2005), as well as the similarly coded masculine figure who bursts through the windshield of the Pingots' car in *Fat Girl*: he wears an oily worker's cap and overalls, the company's logo lacking specificity since it is partly obscured by wear and dirt; there is grime under his fingernails; and his face, repulsively sweaty, is almost always obscured by his cap, by backlighting, or by the framing of the shot.

Marie seems like Carol Clover's Final Girl until the revelation about her psychosis. Typically, when the Final Girl defeats the killer, "we are triumphant" because "she is by any measure the slasher film's hero" (Clover 45). Certainly we feel this for a fleeting moment in *High Tension*, as Marie suffocates the killer; but it is precisely at this moment of her triumph that we discover she is *also* the monster, and we fear for Alex anew rather than feel relief for her safety. When Marie returns to "rescue" Alex, the scene looks much like Clover's description: "By the time the drama has played itself out, darkness yields to light (typically as day breaks) and the close quarters of the barn (closet, elevator, attic, basement) give way to the open expanse of the yard (field, road, lakescape, cliff)" (49). In *High Tension*, it is indeed morning, the sunshine beaming promisingly over a lushly green rural landscape and into the back of the truck, its doors flung open to the fresh air—but in this film, even the light of day brings no peace from the torments of difference.

3

NATURAL MONSTERS

As society become more urbanized and technological, we become more estranged from nature. Consider, for example, how we get our food. The number of family farms has been shrinking steadily for decades, and today most people in the First World get their meat and produce from franchise supermarkets, often prepackaged and bulk purchased rather than locally sourced. Online websites choose our menus, select the ingredients, and send them neatly packaged to our home. We neither hunt nor prepare our own meat and fish; the butchering of animals and treatment of livestock, fowl, and farmed fish takes place in massive plants, largely hidden away from public view. As a result, we romanticize nature as a separate and distinct space, a place of peaceful beauty where we can "get away from it all."

Our uncomfortable unfamiliarity with nature is expressed by the numerous monster movies about city folk who encounter monstrous inbred rednecks and Satanists once they venture into rural America, such as *The Devil's Rain* (1975), *Race with the Devil* (1975), *The Blair Witch Project* (1999), and the *Wrong Turn* series (2003–14). Even as we feel threatened by the mysteries of nature, we find it comforting to sentimentalize it and to imagine nature as something beyond the corrupting influences of contemporary life. But nature is not like a Disney documentary, with cute anthropomorphic animals spunkily protecting their families; rather, it is, to quote Tennyson, "red in tooth and claw," a constant struggle for survival in a complexly interdependent and increasingly challenged food chain.

At the same time, we have grown more aware of environmental pollution and global warming as we have seen their dramatic effects around the globe and learned hard lessons about the complex interconnections of the ecosystem. Several significant events beginning in the 1960s helped spur awareness and concern about pollution, as well as animate environmental activism, beginning with the publication of Rachel Carson's *Silent Spring* in 1962, a nonfiction warning about the use of pesticides that became a national best seller. In 1969, the Cuyahoga River in Ohio, which feeds into Lake Erie, was so polluted that it caught fire; the fire became a national media event. In the next decade, the discovery of environmental pollution and its linkage to cancers and other serious health problems was confirmed in the residents of the Love Canal neighborhood of Niagara Falls, New York. Ironically, the neighborhood had been envisioned originally as a model city of the future, but it was built on a site that for a decade had served as a dumping ground for toxic waste from a local chemical company. In the movies, monsters were now literally lurking in our backyards.

MONSTROUS FAUNA AND FLORA

It is hardly coincidental that the same period that saw a rise in both environmental disasters and ecological awareness also generated a cycle of environmental monster movies. *Swamp Thing* (1982) and *The Toxic Avenger* (1984) both depict humans hideously transformed by toxic waste. Military experimentation, whether active or long abandoned, is often the cause of natural monsters such as the mutant fish of *Piranha* (1984), as is industrial pollution, which is the cause of the mutant killer bear in *Prophecy* (1979), the killer ants in *Empire of the Ants* (1977), and the parasites in *The Bay* (2012). Dubbed by Andrew Tudor "natural nasties" that show a "'mad'—or, at least, angry—nature" (61), the monstrous animals in these films often seek to enact revenge on humanity for its wanton destruction of nature. In *Frogs* (1972)— "cold green skin against soft warm flesh . . . a croak . . . a scream!" promised the film's poster—a variety of reptiles and insects team up to kill the authoritarian plantation owner (Ray Milland) who is wantonly poisoning his land with pesticide.

M. Night Shyamalan's *The Happening* (2008) depicts a bloody revenge by a united front of flora. In this film, the very grasses on which we unthinkingly tread rise up in protest. The attack begins in New York City's Central Park, where, as we later find out, the concentration of vegetation has released a deadly neurotoxin into the air that causes people to commit suicide. The attack spreads throughout the northeastern United States, killing millions. The film's bewildered and frightened characters offer a multitude of explanations for the attack—terrorism, bacteria, a nuclear leak—and at one point, there is a telling shot of a greenhouse in the foreground and a nuclear power plant in the background. But the film withholds any clear and simple explanation for the phenomenon. Throughout, protagonist Elliot Moore (Mark Wahlberg) tries to employ scientific observation and reasoning to determine the cause of the attack and how to survive it; but in the coda, three months after the attack ends and life has returned to normal, an expert on television responds to a question about the cause by concluding, "It was an act of nature, and we'll never understand it." In the final scene, the same phenomenon seems to be beginning in a Paris park.

Perhaps, as Drake Douglas would contend, a film like *The Happening* demonstrates that science has answered too much, that we have already unlocked the secrets of nature, and that we still need to feel a sense of mystery in its presence (11). The same might be said of Hitchcock's *The Birds* (1963), about a series of inexplicable bird attacks on a small California town. The film's opening scene in a pet shop, where animals have been tamed for our pleasure, is a space devoted to the seeming domestication of nature. But Hitchcock soon disturbs our civilized comfort—he famously said that the film is about "complacency" (Hitchcock 300).

As the plot unfolds, Melanie Daniels (Tippi Hedren) flirtatiously pursues lawyer Mitch Brenner (Rod Taylor) from the San Francisco pet shop where they first meet to the small town of Bodega Bay, where he lives with his daughter, Cathy (Veronica Cartwright), and possessive mother, Lydia (Jessica Tandy). Melanie rents a rowboat to take her across the bay to the Brenners' house, where she plans to leave a pair of lovebirds she bought at the pet shop as a gift for Mitch. As she rows back across the bay to the town, Mitch having discovered her prank and watching from shore, the first bird attack comes: a quick swoop of a small gull that pecks Melanie in the head and draws blood. Mitch comes to Melanie's aid, and the bird attacks escalate from then on, eventually forcing Melanie and the Brenners to barricade themselves in the house, now prisoners of the birds and a reversal of the situation in the pet shop. Radio reports tell of attacks spreading to nearby communities, and in the film's final shot, Mitch leads the women slowly to his car through a landscape filled with perched birds of many species apparently massing for the next attack. They drive away to an uncertain future, leaving the image filled with birds but now devoid of people.

As with *The Happening*, *The Birds* offers no explanation for the avian attacks. In the key scene in the local restaurant, where Mitch takes Melanie after the first attack, an ornithologist makes it clear that normally birds of different feathers do not flock together. While the conversation about the birds' mysterious behavior occurs, we hear a server place orders for fried chicken, hinting that this threat may be nature's deliberate revenge on humanity. Alternatively, we might read the monstrous birds as metaphoric of the characters' repressed tensions: the attacks begin in Bodega Bay when Melanie comes to town, her arrival also triggering the jealousy of Mitch's former girlfriend, local schoolteacher Annie Hayworth (Suzanne Pleshette), who is still in love with Mitch, and the possessiveness of Mitch's mother, a widow whose wish to hold onto her son recalls the domineering Mrs. Bates of *Psycho*. Indeed, a frightened woman in the restaurant explicitly accuses Melanie of being responsible for the attacks.

Whatever the explanation for the avian aggression, *The Birds* emphasizes, like so many apocalyptic films to follow, how tenuous civilization is, how quickly it breaks down and people regress to savagery. When the birds attack the town, before Hitchcock cuts to the famous high-angle ("bird's-eye point of view"?) shot looking down at the destruction, it is shocking to see how fast utter chaos erupts. In a gas station, one man, strafed by birds, drops the pump hose while filling his car's gas tank; gas spills on the ground; another customer unknowingly lights a cigarette and drops a match; the place explodes in a hellish ball of flame. People flee in all directions, helpless. In the sobering opinion of the town drunk, also in the restaurant, "It's the end of the world."

Hitchcock subtly emphasizes the precarious nature of our social order, beginning with Melanie out in the open bay, a city fish out of water as it were, exposed and lacking solid grounding underfoot. As Melanie reaches to her head to check her injury after that first peck, Hitchcock cuts to a close-up of her hand, her pale glove stained bright red by blood at the fingertips. The stark color contrast of this image is graphically startling and metaphorically suggests the potential violence underlying the veneer of civilized society. Later in the film, Hitchcock uses a related image similarly: before Lydia discovers the body of her neighbor Dan Fawcett, she first sees a row of shattered teacups hanging in the pantry when she enters his house, a clear sign that something is amiss.

The monstrous consequences of ecological imbalance also inform *Wolfen* (1981), with its plot involving a New York City detective, Dewey Wilson (Albert Finney), investigating a series of grisly murders including that of a wealthy real-estate tycoon in the process of building a new complex in lower Manhattan. As Wilson eventually discovers, the murders are being committed by a pack of wolf-like creatures who kill to protect what remains of their hunting grounds. In the climax, the wolfen kill Wilson's partner and surround him in the tycoon's penthouse. When Wilson destroys the scale model of the proposed real-estate development, the wolfen realize that he is not their enemy, back off, and disappear. The wolfen are associated with Native Americans, who bring their appreciation for nature and the land to an understanding of and respect for the creatures. A similar theme informs *The Burrowers*, involving predatory creatures that move under the ground. This horror western begins like John Ford's classic western *The Searchers* (1956), with several pioneer women seemingly kidnapped by Indians and a search party of men organized to pursue and rescue them. As it turns out, the women have not been taken by Indians but have been snatched and cocooned by the burrowers for eating later, after rot sets in and softens their bodies. We learn from a Native American that the burrowers used to feed on buffalo, but now that the white man has exterminated them, the burrowers have had to find another source of food—meaning humans. In the brutally ironic ending of the film, the vain and racist cavalry officer, modeled on General George Armstrong Custer, misconstrues the danger because of his own racist perspective and hangs the only Native American who knows the secret of the poison that paralyzes the burrowers until dawn, when exposure to the sun will kill them like vampires. *The Burrowers* uses the western, with its traditionally racist view of indigenous cultures and white expansionism, to offer a devastating critique of capitalist greed and racism. The United States will never exorcize its demons, *The Burrowers* suggests, without unearthing its violently racist past.

ATOMIC MONSTERS

At the end of World War II, humanity was quickly thrust into a new world in which nothing less than utter annihilation was suddenly possible. Radioactivity posed a new kind of invisible threat with unforetold consequences even as Cold War tensions were mounting. All public buildings had designated fallout shelters, and schoolchildren practiced superfluous duck-and-cover drills.

In the movies, the anxieties of the atomic era were frequently expressed in the form of rampaging monsters. Also, people experienced monstrous mutations as a result of exposure to atomic blasts: an H-bomb test turned Tor Johnson into *The Beast of Yucca Flats* (1961), while Dr. Gil McKenna (Robert Clarke) became *The Hideous Sun Demon* (1959), a scaly reptilian creature when exposed to sunlight. Scott Carey (Grant Williams) became *The Incredible Shrinking Man* (1957) and Glenn Langlan (Glenn Manning) *The Amazing Colossal Man* (1957). The latter, reaching the size of an elephant, tries to turn to his Bible for comfort, but he is now so large that the holy book is too small for him to read: not even religion can provide solace against the awesome destructive power of the Bomb.

Nuclear fear was also embodied at the time in the plethora of monsters that took wing and tunneled, crawled and climbed their way through similar plots featuring scenes of mass destruction, fleeing citizens, and the deployment of military personnel and hardware. This monstrous menagerie included giant ants (*Them!*), arachnids (*Tarantula* [1955], *The Black Scorpion* [1957]), grasshoppers (*Beginning of the End* [1957]), squids (*It Came from Beneath the Sea* [1955]), crustaceans (*Attack of the Crab Monsters* [1957], *The Monster That Challenged the World* [1957]), and an absurd-looking alien flying creature that resembles *Sesame Street*'s Big Bird scalded by acid (*The Giant Claw* [1957]). The pinnacles of human civilization amounts to nothing against the potential devastation of nuclear weapons—as signified by the frequent shots in these movies of monsters destroying famous landmarks, from the East Coast (the Cyclone roller coaster at Coney Island in New York City in *The Beast from 20,000 Fathoms* [1953]) to the West Coast (the Golden Gate Bridge in *It Came from Beneath the Sea*).

In many of these movies, the monstrous creatures are extinct dinosaurs whose ageless slumber was disturbed by atomic testing ("They were never really dead. They just slept," explains a scientist in *Rodan* [1956]) or mutations of natural creatures created by atomic testing. The monstrous ants of *Them!* are not only giant but have become bloodthirsty carnivores, as have the mutated giant scorpions in *The Black Scorpion*. In *Them!*, when the heroes find the giant ants' nest, we see a high-angle shot from their perspective in a helicopter looking down at its mounded entrance as an ant emerges and rolls a human ribcage down the hill. A similar discovery is made by Japanese scientists in a helicopter in *Rodan*. The lesson in these films was obvious: it was the dawn of the nuclear age; people had seen the devastation caused by the atomic bomb attacks on Hiroshima and Nagasaki only a decade earlier. Still, these giant-monster movies betrayed an ambivalence about atomic power and the science that harnessed it: they often climaxed with the monster being destroyed by a new weapon, as in both *The Beast from 20,000 Fathoms* and the Japanese film *Gojira* (1954). As Peter Biskind points out, "Many of the monsters of fifties sci-fi were at least partially attributable to science; nevertheless, where science caused the problem, science often solved it too" (104).

Gojira (reedited and released for American exhibition as *Godzilla, King of the Monsters* in 1956) replays the traumatic horrors of nuclear war for the only country to have experienced atomic attack. It begins with an assault by a giant prehistoric creature on a Japanese fishing boat, a scene inspired by an actual event a few months before the making of the film, involving a Japanese fishing vessel caught in a U.S. nuclear test of a hydrogen bomb on Bikini Atoll. As authorities in *Gojira* soon discover, the creature is radioactive, leaving traces of radiation in its wake and survivors of its rampages suffering from radiation burns, playing on contemporary fears of nuclear fallout and contamination of fish stocks. Combining elements of a tyrannosaurus, a stegosaurus, an alligator, and a mythical dragon, Godzilla was inspired by Ray Harryhausen's fictional rhedosaurus in *The Beast from 20,000 Fathoms*, which is similarly radioactive: in that film, as the military tracks the wounded creature through the evacuated streets of New York City, the soldiers succumb to radiation poisoning emanating from giant drops of its blood. Godzilla's attack on Tokyo, an extended sequence of mass destruction involving a clever mix of model work, stop-motion, matte shots, and an actor (stuntman Haruo Nakajima, who played the creature in eleven of the sequels) in a latex monster suit, turns the city into a blazing inferno generated by the creature's atomic breath that cannot help but recall the destruction wrought by the two atomic bomb drops in Japan just a few years before. Because these films were made early in the atomic era and before the end of the Cold War, they were suggestively open-ended even as they seemed to provide comfortable narrative closure with the death of the creature. At the end of *Godzilla*, recalling the end of *Them!* and several other monster movies of the period, humanity's apparent victory is qualified as the characters wonder whether the continued testing of nuclear weapons will unleash further mutated monsters on the world.

Recognized by Guinness World Records as the longest continuously running movie franchise, *Gojira* was instrumental in the creation of the *kaiju eiga* (Japanese for "strange beast"), or giant-monster movie. Guillermo del Toro's more recent *Pacific Rim* (2013) builds on the *kaiju eiga* films—the scene in which Mako Mori (Rinko Kikuchi) remembers her traumatic past cowering in fear with her mother from a *kaiju* attack is a direct reference to *Gojira*—but is more upbeat in its message. Del Toro's film is set in 2013 (the year of the film's release, suggesting these events could happen "tomorrow"), after a rift develops between two tectonic plates in the depths of the Pacific Ocean through which different giant monsters are emerging at periodic intervals, wreaking havoc on the coastal areas of Pacific countries. As we discover later when a scientist mentally joins with one of the *kaiju*, the creatures are actually bioweapons created by a race of aliens as a first wave of invasion, to eliminate the human "vermin," as one of the scientists puts it. To fight off the *kaiju*, "the world came together, pooling its resources and throwing aside all rivalries for the sake of the greater good," explains Raleigh Beckett (Charlie Hunnam) in voice-over at the beginning.

MICROSCOPIC AND MINIATURE MONSTERS

Today we are as much concerned about chemical and bioweapons as we are about nuclear weapons. Chemical weapons have been around since World War I, but fears about them have been stoked by their recent documented use in war-ravaged Syria and by the appearance in recent years of new diseases like Legionnaire's disease, Norwalk virus, N1H1 (bird flu), swine flu, SARS, West Nile virus,

Lyme disease, and, of course, AIDS, not to mention what seems like weekly recalls of processed foods because of possible infections like listeria, salmonella, and other food-borne diseases. *Nosferatu* (1922) associates the vampire with the plague through rats. *The Satan Bug* (1965) and *The Andromeda Strain* (1971) were early films about biological threats, and the more recent spate of zombie movies, in which the undead state is induced inadvertently by experiments in virology, speak to the same anxieties. The zombie plague in *The Return of the Living Dead* (1985) is caused by leakage from canisters of a military chemical weapon kept in storage.

Monstrous microbes are so frightening precisely because they cannot be seen but nevertheless are capable of penetrating the body. The monster in Steven Soderbergh's *Contagion* (2011) is a new viral mutation that, as we learn at the very end of the film, developed when a pig consumed infected bat guano before it was butchered for a restaurant. The virus jumps from the unwashed hands of the restaurant chef to Beth Emhoff (Gwyneth Paltrow), a corporate executive celebrating the end of a successful business trip in Hong Kong. As Patient Zero, Emhoff spreads the virus rapidly, and within months, it kills one-twelfth of the world's population (reference is made several times in the film to the deadly influenza outbreak of 1918). Symptoms appear quickly, beginning with a cough and flu-like aches and advancing within days to convulsions and coma.

The film's style brilliantly captures the inevitable and uncontrollable spread of such an outbreak. It frequently interrupts the narrative with montages of the spreading disease; the quick editing, accompanied by Cliff Martinez's insistently rhythmical electronic score, emphasizes its inexorable spread given the interconnecting mobility of society today. People are seen touching shared public surfaces everywhere they go and everything they do. The film begins immediately with one of these montages (the credits are withheld until the film's end), initiated by a cough on the soundtrack but without dialogue for its duration. We see Beth using touchscreens and exchanging documents at the restaurant and airport and others unwittingly following and thereby spreading the virus to other cities around the globe.

In the film's narrative structure, *Contagion* recalls the disaster-film cycle of the late 1970s, such as *The Poseidon Adventure* (1972) and *The Towering Inferno* (1974): a calamitous event occurs that threatens a band of survivors, some of whom die as they attempt to survive while others live. In the disaster films, the characters' moral qualities are irrelevant to their fate, as is their status as stars, and the same holds true for *Contagion*. The dedicated scientist Dr. Erin Mears (Kate Winslet), fighting the virus on the front lines, succumbs to the infection and dies a lonely death, unable to be evacuated because of bureaucracy, while the sleazy, opportunistic blogger (Jude Law) not only survives but profits substantially from endorsing a bogus cure on his website. The first person we see in the film is Gwyneth Paltrow, a likeable star, but she is soon killed off. As we come to understand the scale of the threat, we are hampered from identifying with any one of the film's numerous stars, as any of them could fall victim to the virus. The later close-up of Paltrow's face followed by its suddenly and shockingly being peeled back from her skull makes us realize after a moment that Beth is dead and that her cadaver is undergoing an autopsy. Like the brutal murder of *Psycho*'s ostensible star, this scene in *Contagion* violates viewers' tacit contract with the star system, amplifying its affective power.

Like *The Birds*, *Contagion* also emphasizes how thin the veneer of civilization is and how quickly it crumbles. Once the epidemic takes hold, an effective montage shows a variety of public and urban spaces now eerily empty of people and populated instead by posters for the missing and impromptu memorials for victims. Mobs of people clash for supplies, and more than once the film suggests that our very natures may hinder humanity in fighting such a rampant and lethal infection, that we may be our own worst monsters.

Contagion also expresses anxiety about governmental bureaucracy, undoubtedly fueled by the problematic response of governmental organizations such as the Federal Emergency Management Agency (FEMA) to Hurricane Katrina in 2005. In the film, no quick and uniform action can be taken by the federal government because, as Dr. Ellis Cheever (Laurence Fishburne) of the Centers for Disease Control explains, each state has its own Department of Health, and consequently there are fifty different outbreak protocols. At one point, doctors and nurses treating the infected go on strike because there are no protocols for dealing with this new infection. When an antidote is finally found, a lottery by birthday is held (recalling the military draft lottery during the height of the Vietnam War) to determine the order in which people will be able to get it. The film's view of the inability of government to act decisively in times of crisis may resonate with contemporary audiences disaffected with gridlock in Washington, but it is a stark contrast to the monster movies of the 1950s, in which, once authorities are convinced of a threat, viewers could rest assured that it would promptly be dealt with. *Contagion* ends with the scientist who found the cure putting a sample of the virus in her lab's cryogenic freezer along with other deadly strains—a reminder, like the ends of the giant monster movies, that the disease may have been defeated this time but that there remains the possibility of its escaping and mutating once again at some time in the future.

Insects are wholly other, inscrutable participants of a selfless collectivity we can neither know nor understand. They challenge our sense of human individuality, as do those monster movies in which humans are absorbed into a collective mentality, as in *Invasion of the Body Snatchers*. The many people with a general phobia of insects (entophobia) or a specific insect phobia—myrmecophobia (fear of ants), apiphobia (fear of bees), and arachnophobia (fear of spiders), for example—would agree with Scott Carey, the contracting protagonist of *The Incredible Shrinking Man*, when he describes the spider he must fight for survival as "the most terrifying [monster] ever beheld by human eyes."

The Hellstrom Chronicle (1971), an early example of mockumentary, combines state-of-the-art microscopic and time-lapse photography with the conventions of both documentary filmmaking and the monster movie to exploit our common fear of insects. It is narrated by a fictitious scientist, Dr. Nils Hellstrom (Lawrence Pressman), who appears as an expert speaking to the camera with the frightened, hushed expression of someone who has stumbled on an elaborate conspiracy theory that spells the doom of the human race. As he talks, astonishing sequences of wasps, ants, termites, mayflies, and other insects are juxtaposed with occasional clips from monster movies like *Them!* Even carnivorous plants are invoked as monstrously frightening. The opening of the later *Empire of the Ants*, about a group of potential home buyers on a real-estate junket who are terrorized by giant ants mutated by radioactive waste, begins in a similar pseudodocumentary manner that might have been lifted from *The Hellstrom Chronicle*. As does the narrator of the later film, Dr. Hellstrom also predicts that insects ultimately will win the battle for survival on Earth because of their adaptability and collective efficiency, unhampered by human individualism. It is, he says, "the unreasoning brutality of nature's plan."

Right from the start, Dr. Hellstrom offers a melodramatic view of the monstrous threat that insects pose to humanity: "With a three-hundred-million-year head start on Man, the insect begins to develop his powers," he ominously notes. "He dominates the earth and exploits his dominion well. With each new generation come new experiments in shape and function, transforming him into specters as limitless as the imagination of the insane." Accompanying this hyperbolic account is a montage of close-ups of different insects' faces, their expressionless and unblinking gazes blankly returning our own. Dr. Hellstrom consistently emphasizes that insects have the advantage of lacking individuality, and at the same time, he uses loaded phrases and adjectives that impute evil intent to insect behavior. Shown in feeding frenzies, their appetites are described as "hideous," mosquitoes are referred to as "the master executioner," a termite mound is described as "a seething house of horrors." Even carnivorous plants like the Venus flytrap are said to have "gaping jaws."

Another montage shows insects killing, dismembering, and consuming each other, like scenes out of *World War Z* (2013) that feature swarms of the undead. Since there is no sense of scale, the microscopic images of insects make them seem huge—a strategy for suggesting a monstrously large size that involves matching close-ups of actual lizards with live-action footage of actors and model work that harks back to *Flash Gordon* (1936), the first science-fiction serial, and then employed in many of the giant-insect monster movies of the 1950s. In terms of adaptability, "we are dwarves, he the giant," asserts Hellstrom of the insect. A shot of insects engaged in life-and-death battle in the soil pans away to reveal their battlefield as part of a lawn in a park on which a pair of young lovers are obliviously reclining, hinting (like the famous opening of David Lynch's *Blue Velvet* [1986]) at the ever-present dangers that lurk beneath nature's seemingly placid surface and of which we are typically blithely unaware.

The battle between humans and insects is literalized, with the help of CGI, in Paul Verhoeven's *Starship*

Troopers (1997), a big-budget adaptation of Robert Heinlein's 1959 novel in which humanity is engaged in an intergalactic war with extraterrestrial intelligent "bugs." The threat the alien bugs pose to the human race is no less dire in *Phase IV* (1974), in which the malevolent ants of one Arizona colony are normal in size but superintelligent, the beneficiaries of an unspecified cosmic event. In this film, two scientists, Ernest Hubbs (Nigel Davenport) and James Lesko (Michael Murphy), set up a portable laboratory near the ant colony to observe them and gather information. Once again big close-ups of the ants, their mandibles working, in conjunction with Lesko's voice-over comments, make them seem threatening and conspiratorial. Time-lapse photography of the ants en masse ambushing and consuming their natural predators shows how they have upset the natural order. When we see ants pulling the body of a dead comrade back through the corridor to the queen so she can ingest the poison sprayed on it in order to develop an immune generation, each toiling ant in turn being replaced as it too succumbs to the poison, or when we witness ants respectfully lining up the bodies of their dead comrades apparently to mourn them, we are chilled by their selfless and deliberate behavior.

As Dr. Hubbs comes to realize how intelligent the ants are—the narrator at the beginning of *Empire of the Ants* warns us not to let their diminutive size fool us—he becomes determined to kill them. Although he observes that the threat they pose is in their mass, not their size, Hubbs feels that his natural place atop the Great Chain of Being is being displaced and resents it. "I am not helpless. I will not be humiliated," he shouts as he tries unsuccessfully to squash a lone ant scout. Determined to show them that "man must not give in," he is brought low by his own vainglory, falling into a trap in the ground prepared for him by the ants, who then swarm over him. The film ends with Lesko sliding into the ants' giant nest, accepting his fate as a guinea pig for them as he says, "We knew then that we were being changed and made part of their world. We didn't know for what purpose . . . but we knew we would be told."

MECHANICAL MONSTERS

It is no coincidence that, as mentioned in chapter 1, books on movie monsters tend to devote a chapter to the "monster," by which they mean Frankenstein's creation, this one monster thus equal to entire species of the creatures of the night such as werewolves and vampires. It is telling, too, that in popular discourse, "Frankenstein" tends to refer to the creature, who is in fact unnamed in both novel and film, rather than to the scientist who made him. (In *Son of Frankenstein* [1939], Basil Rathbone as Baron Wolf von

Frankenstein complains about just this semantic confusion.) It indicates our intense interest in monsters, and it is also ironically appropriate, for Dr. Henry Frankenstein (Colin Clive) is himself a monster—not only as a mad scientist conducting unholy experiments but because he presumes to usurp the power of God by creating life. In this sense, the mise-en-scène of the laboratory—clearly influenced by Rotwang's in *Metropolis*—with its bizarre Bunsen burners, cackling electrodes, Tesla coils, and other impressive electrical devices, represents not only the dark supernatural world of the Gothic as opposed to that of enlightened scientific inquiry but also Frankenstein's unhinged mind. The slab with the reposing creature, elevated to the stormy sky, suggests that the doctor's overreaching extends toward heaven itself. "I made it with my own hands," he tells Dr. Waldman; his fiancée, Elizabeth; and his friend Victor. "It's alive," he exults. "Now I know what it feels like to be God."

In short, Dr. Frankenstein commits the cardinal sin imagined by scientists in monster fiction: he has gone, as the cliché moral of so many movies has it, where humanity was not meant to go. For Andrew Tudor, "The belief that science is dangerous is as central to the horror movie as is a belief in the malevolent inclinations of ghosts, ghouls, vampires and zombies" (133), and this fear is typically embodied in the stereotyped figure of the mad scientist. In Fritz Lang's *Metropolis*, Rotwang (Rudolf Klein-Rogge), the scientist who creates the robot Maria, is associated more with the mystic arts than scientific method, just as Dr. Morbius in *Forbidden Planet* changes his costume toward the end to what resembles an alchemist's robe. In *Son of Frankenstein*, Baron Wolf von Frankenstein receives a letter from his father, Henry Frankenstein, which says, "If you, like me, burn with the irresistible desire to penetrate the unknown, carry on. Even though the path is cruel and tortuous, carry on. Like every seeker after truth you will be hated, blasphemed, and condemned." So Dr. Janos Rukh (Bela Lugosi) in *The Invisible Ray* (1936) turns mad from radiation poisoning, even though his intentions had been beneficial, because he pushes the boundaries of science beyond the "natural" (that is, the known). When, in *The Alligator People* (1959), the patient (Richard Crane) who is unintentionally turned into a reptile by an experimental medication tells his physician, Mark Sinclair (George Macready), "You're not God. You can't know everything," Dr. Sinclair responds, "I feel like I've been playing at it. And now I'm being punished for it." And, of course, he is—killed in his lab as it explodes in the climax. As Tudor notes, whether mad scientists want to rule the world or unleash unintended horrors on the world, "either way, science gets the blame" (133).

New areas of scientific research often generate fear and uncertainty regarding their implications and morality. Nuclear power, cloning, virtual reality, and so on have all been made monstrous in the movies. Rogue robots and AIs are plentiful on the big screen, as are dangerous computers. The question of machine sentience—artificial intelligence—is a fearful one for those, like Dr. Hubbs in *Phase IV*, who regard human beings as unique because of consciousness. Even the development and use of antibiotics to treat infection, now commonplace in medicine, can call forth the monstrous when they were relatively new in 1956, the year *Bigger than Life* appeared. In the film, high school teacher Ed Avery (James Mason) exceeds his prescribed dosage of cortisone for pain management and becomes a delusional monster threatening to sacrifice his young son to God like Abraham until he is forcibly stopped by a neighbor.

In *Colossus: The Forbin Project* (1970), the scientist becomes the victim of the monster computer he created—an updated variation of *Frankenstein* for the dawn of the cybernetic age—despite his insistence, like Hubbs's, that humanity is the master. Dr. Charles Forbin (Eric Braeden) is the chief designer of Colossus, a new government supercomputer built into the side of a mountain to make it impervious to attack. As soon as the machine goes online, it detects a similar system, Guardian, built by the

Soviet Union, that also has just been activated, and both systems demand to be able to communicate with the other. The two computers, controlling their respective country's nuclear missiles, threaten nuclear attack unless their demands are met. Once connected, the two computers start to exchange information, beginning with simple mathematical equations but soon growing exponentially more complex to the point of surpassing the knowledge of their human creators. When the two governments decide to terminate the computer link, each machine responds by launching missiles at targets in the other country. The communications link is begrudgingly restored by the governments, and (because it is an American film, presumably) Colossus intercepts and destroys the Soviet missile heading for Texas, although the American weapon detonates, destroying a populated area of the USSR.

The Colossus/Guardian entity, now in control, orders the installation of surveillance cameras and a voice synthesizer to replace its printed readouts. Earlier, the absence of a voice made the machine seem more menacing, but any inclination toward humanizing Colossus once it is able to speak is thwarted by the computer's deliberate choice to sound mechanical. Colossus imprisons its creator in his apartment, needing him to implement its plans to design another computer that will supersede itself, while both governments seek to defuse their missiles—to disarm "this monster," as one of the president's staff says—without the computers knowing. But the machines detect the ruse and detonate two missiles in their silos—"so that you will learn by experience that I do not tolerate interference," as Colossus explains. As the film ends, Colossus goes public, globally telecasting a message from the ominously named "World Control" that humanity has a choice between a new millennium of world peace under its reign, fulfilling what it was designed to do, or mass destruction.

The film's deadpan style eerily matches the cold logic of Colossus. Forbin warns others not to "personalize" it. "The next step is deification." But the most chilling aspect of this horrifying scenario is that Colossus is less of a rogue machine than one doing its job with efficiency. As it points out, it has quickly achieved its purpose of bringing an end to war. Colossus goes about its work completely indifferent to the fate of individual humans, such as those it killed in the silo explosions. When Colossus announces its five-year plan for the building of a next-generation giant computer on the island of Crete, it tells Forbin that the island's population will need to be quickly relocated; Forbin protests about the impossible scale of the evacuation, but Colossus ominously replies that humans will have to find a solution or it will do so for them. Lacking compassion and human understanding,

Colossus regulates every aspect of Forbin's life, including the frequency and time for his sexual activity. As the film ends, Colossus tells Forbin, "in time you will come to regard me not only with respect and awe but with love," to which Forbin responds, "Never!" However, in the shots of people around the world listening to the voice of Colossus, we see a young boy wearing a T-shirt with the logo of World Control—suggesting that the first generation of human life under the computer is already well under way. When Forbin realizes the extent of what his work has wrought, he makes the film's cautionary moral explicit in his assertion that "*Frankenstein* should be required reading for every scientist."

MARTIAN MONSTERS

Extraterrestrials are rarely treated as unthreatening, as creatures with whom we should try to understand and communicate. The aliens of Jack Arnold's *It Came from Outer Space* (1953) just need time to repair their ship; and the alien intelligence of *The Space Children* (1958), also directed by Arnold, takes over the children of parents stationed at a government rocket-testing facility for, as we eventually learn, the less-than-nefarious purpose of sabotaging the rockets in order to prevent the mutual assured destruction of an imminent World War III.

Steven Spielberg's E.T. is like a cuddly stuffed animal who just wants to go home, appropriate for a family-oriented science fiction movie. Also, just as the western has evolved from demonizing its generic other, the "Indian," so science-fiction cinema has done the same with the alien. So in *District 9* (2009), the crustacean-looking aliens are kept in ghettos and are referred to with the racist epithet "prawn" as an obvious comment on real-world racism.

Arrival (2016) is, on one level, about our tendency to automatically regard an alien life form, which is almost certain to be physically different from us, as monstrous. The aliens in the film are not monsters, although they look like it: squid-like giants ("heptapods") floating in the air with eight tentacles tipped with powerful suction cups. Creatures with tentacles, like the alien brain in *Invaders from Mars* (1954), the giant octopus of *It Conquered the World* (1956), or the giant squid of *20,000 Leagues under the Sea* (1954), induce fears of smothering and entrapment. However, the heptapods of *Arrival*, nicknamed Abbott and Costello by physicist Ian Donnelly (Jeremy Renner), are in fact gentle creatures who have come offering to humanity the "tool" of their language, which allows them to perceive across time, in return for our helping them in some unspecified way in three thousand years. Heptapod ships have landed in twelve countries, each country assembling a team of scientists to establish communication with the aliens. As the different groups begin to make progress, they become more suspicious of each other and covetous of their own knowledge gleaned thus far; eventually they all break off contact, no longer working together, and tensions escalate to the point of global war. The film shows how the primary human reaction to the alien other is one of fear.

Apart from a few such examples, though, the majority of movie aliens have presented alien life forms as unambiguously monstrous. The very term "alien" indicates their irrevocable otherness, the double meaning of the term as "foreigner" played on in *Alien Nation* (1988), in which humanoid aliens live in ghettos but have begun integrating into human society. The film uses the integrated buddy cop format of movies like *48 Hrs.* (1982) in teaming a human cop with an alien on a murder case. *The Thing*, one of the movies that launched the science fiction movie boom of the 1950s, is paradigmatic: its alien, clearly intelligent and capable of interplanetary travel, is portrayed as a grunting bloodthirsty monster. When a group of humans make first contact with aliens in the movies, there is frequently one character, often a misguided scientist like Dr. Carrington in *The Thing*, who tries to communicate and convey his friendly intentions—and usually such figures are the first to die at the hands (or tentacles or disintegrating ray) of the aliens. In Tobe Hooper's remake of *Invaders from Mars* (1986), the scientist from SETI (Search for Extraterrestrial Intelligence), played by the baby-faced Bud Cort, is the first victim of the invasion. Scotty the journalist's dire warning at the end of the first version of *The Thing* to "keep watching the skies!"— as the shot shows his face looking up in trepidation— articulates the dominant view of aliens in the movies. This explicit xenophobia is reiterated in *Life* in the final voice-over monologue, a log recording by the biologist of the doomed International Space Station crew warning future space explorers to be wary of any and all new life-forms that they might discover out there.

The first people to attempt contact in H. G. Wells's novel *The War of the Worlds* are promptly incinerated, as also happens in the first film adaptation in 1953. With the film's setting transposed from Britain to California, it drew heavily on Cold War anxieties. In the climax, nuclear scientist Clayton Forrester (Gene Barry) and love interest Sylvia Van Buren (Ann Robinson) take what they assume is final refuge, as the Martian war machines with their heat rays are laying waste to San Francisco, in a church along with a group of other civilians fleeing the destruction. Suddenly, as if in answer to their prayers, the alien machines shut down, and the Martians all die because they lacked resistance to microbes, the smallest creatures that, as the narrator informs us, God "in his wisdom" placed on Earth. The two worlds in conflict are Earth and Mars but also the Free World and the Communist World, the latter of which gets its comeuppance with defeat for its godlessness.

The second version, directed by Steven Spielberg and released in 2005, just four years after 9/11, shifts the fears, this time from the Cold War to the War on Terror. Perhaps its biggest departure from Wells's original tale is the premise that, rather than arriving in capsules shot across space, here the Martian machines have been buried under the earth for eons, animated by aliens parachuted into them like terrorist "sleeper" cells under our very noses that are suddenly awakened. The attack begins in New York City, site of the 9/11 attacks on the World Trade Center, and then spreads to the world beyond. A downed passenger jetliner that crashes onto a house in which protagonist Ray Ferry (Tom Cruise) and his children are hiding is a resonant image for post-9/11 consciousness; indeed, Ray's son, Robbie (Justin Chatwin), explicitly asks if the attack is the work of terrorists. Once on Earth, the Martians quickly begin transforming the environment into their habitat, expressing the fear that Muslims are unable or unwilling to assimilate into American society, that they want to maintain certain institutions in the United States such as sharia law. The significant differences between the two film versions of H. G. Wells's classic invasion narrative vividly demonstrate how monster movies shape their aliens to express and exploit topical fears.

4

SUPERNATURAL MONSTERS

We are simultaneously attracted to and horrified by the supernatural, an unknown realm—whether it is "the astral plane" of *Insidious* (2010) or "the sunken place" of *Get Out*—that includes whatever cannot be explained by science and the physical laws of nature as we know them. People watch frightening stories involving ghosts, demons, and devils even as they seek out spiritualists and fortune tellers because we fear the finality of death but hope nonetheless that there is something after. The manifestation of supernatural beings through religion, superstition, magic, or the inexplicable in a world recognizably our own usually implies a tone of horror and the potential appearance of the monstrous. The very existence of supernatural monsters, writes Bruce Kawin, "renders the world an unsettling, unsettled and otherworldly place" (91).

Deriving from the earlier tradition of Gothic fiction, many horror films seem to posit haunted spaces and supernatural presences, only to be eventually resolved as caused by human agency, as in, for example, William Castle's *House on Haunted Hill* (1959), in which it is revealed in the climax that Frederick Loren (Vincent Price) is responsible for the apparent supernatural events as part of a plan to exact revenge against his unfaithful wife. But movies, because the camera has the ability both to show the physical world through the impartiality of the camera lens and to enhance or alter it through the use of optical tricks (reverse motion, superimposition, double exposure, matting, and so on) and special effects (including computer-generated imagery), can create credible worlds that are, in effect, *super*natural. Thus, it is no surprise that cinema has been fascinated with the supernatural from the beginning. Georges Méliès, who was a magician before becoming a filmmaker, was drawn to the phantasmagoric and made numerous films featuring various supernatural creatures. The aforementioned *The Devil's Castle* (1896) featured a vampire, ghosts, a skeleton, witches, and, as one contemporary film catalogue put it, the "Evil One" (Hammond 31).

Even before cinema, the fad of spirit photography developed in the late nineteenth century. With these images, also known at the time as "evidential survival pictures," charlatans sought to convince skeptics and to bilk believers in the hereafter by showing supposed documentary evidence in support of their claims regarding visitations by the dearly departed (Gettings 5). In John Carpenter's *Prince of Darkness*, Professor Birack (Howard Wong) says, when learning about the secret society of priests that have guarded the embodiment of evil for centuries, "The outside world doesn't want to hear that kind of bullshit." But given so many movies about the existence of the supernatural in one form or another, it would seem that audiences certainly do, for supernatural monster movies speak to our anxieties regarding life and death and questions of faith in an increasingly secular and materialist world.

MONSTROUS MANIFESTATIONS

Monster movies tilt away from science fiction and toward horror when they rely on superstition and spiritual faith for their explanation of material phenomena. This tonal shift often happens in adaptations of science-fiction novels because, as Nicholas Ruddick observes, filmmakers tend to aim for the "intensification of affective elements at the expense of intellectual elements" (37). This tension between "the agnostic-rational frame of sf" and the "quasi-theological frame of supernatural horror" (37) is itself at the core of Fritz Lieber's 1943 novel *Conjure Wife* and the three films based on it (*Weird Woman* [1944], *Burn, Witch, Burn!* [1962], and *Witches' Brew* [1980]). The narrator of Lieber's story is Norman Saylor, a skeptical sociology professor who discovers that his wife, Tansy, is in fact a witch and that his career is being controlled by her and other witches, the wives of his competitive colleagues at the college. The fact that the protagonist is a professor foregrounds the importance of his rational worldview and the horror of its consequent destruction when confronted with the reality of magic, which, he learns, has as much to do with his successful career as does the brilliance of any research he might have done. (His name, Norman, like that of the killer in Hitchcock's *Psycho*, connotes the normal, the conventional world we think we know.) The story plays on male fears of women, to be sure, as Saylor learns that the women around him are all secret conspirators battling spells and shaping the destiny of their husbands, but it also firmly associates the masculine with reason and science and femininity with mysticism and magic.

The same tension between science and faith informs *Prince of Darkness*, a tale about the devil, imprisoned in the form of a viscous rotating green liquid in an antique beaker, reawakening after two thousand years and about to be unleashed on the world. The film follows several university scientists and a group of their graduate students who come to study the strange phenomenon of an apparently sentient liquid that has been hidden away in the basement of an abandoned church. The university team is led by the aforementioned Professor Birack, who at the beginning of the film portentously lectures his graduate students in physics, "While order does exist in the universe, it's not what we had in mind." What follows illustrates his thesis, as Satan turns out to be an "anti-God" composed of anti-matter existing in a parallel universe accessible through mirrors. As the plot unfolds over the course of one day and night at the site, one by one the researchers, isolated in part by their worldly cynicism, have their humanity destroyed. The liquid seeps out of the ancient container and infects one of the researchers, who becomes a zombie that kills or infects most of the others. In the climax, one of the students sacrifices herself by jumping through a mirror, holding onto another student who has been impregnated by Satan's bilious fluid, thus preventing the Evil One from emerging into our world—at least for now.

In Tod Browning's 1931 version of *Dracula*, Dr. Van Helsing (Edward Van Sloan) is able to determine the truth about what is going on and so defeat the vampire by combining science and religion. Van Helsing requires empirical evidence and accepts it even when it leads to the supernatural without dismissing the idea as superstitious nonsense. The same is true of Dr. Saunders (Gilbert Emery), the physician who reaches the same conclusion in *The Return of the Vampire* (1943). As he says, the threat "goes deeper than medicine, deeper even than science." By contrast, *Prince of Darkness* continually emphasizes the gap between science and religion, a liminal space where the Devil thrives. When a nun comes to the campus to deliver the request for help to Dr. Birack from a frightened priest (Donald Pleasance), everyone she walks by turns to look at her apparently unusual presence in the hallowed but secular halls of academe, and the students hypothesize that they must be arranging for a sequel to a symposium held years ago on the place of religion in science. The setting of the unassuming church on a busy street with cars continually rushing by and the fact that no one notices that the research group is under siege by street people (spearheaded by Alice Cooper!) drawn by the seductive power of Satan show how removed from faith society has become.

The Fallen (1998) sets up a similar dichotomy. In the plot, Philadelphia police detective John Hobbes (Denzel Washington), working a series of bizarre and inexplicable murders, discovers that a demon, a fallen angel named Azazel, is real and inhabits humans, making them commit violent and criminal acts as it pleases. Azazel has the ability to move from person to person by the merest of physical touches, making it, like the rogue alien in *The Hidden*, nearly impossible to catch, especially in crowds. But Hobbes works out an ingenious plan to entrap it in his own body after poisoning himself and luring it to an isolated area with no one else around for miles. Hobbes is forced to carry out his unsuccessful plan by himself, in secret, having been relieved of duty because no one believes his story. His partner, Jonesy (John Goodman), has the feeling that they are "dealing with shit that ain't in the manual," while his superior, Lieutenant Stanton (Donald Sutherland), says, "People want the world to make sense."

Hobbes's names refers to John Hobbes, author of the influential political treatise *Leviathan* (1651), who argued for the necessity of strong government because of the brutal natural state of humanity, which he described as "a war of all against all." Azazel, in other words, only makes explicit the murderous selfishness that according to the film already resides in everyone. This suggests that the detective Hobbes can never succeed in destroying Azazel, and indeed in the end, the demon escapes through a twist of fate (it enters the body of a cat that happens to pass by the dying Hobbes). The demon is associated with the music of the Rolling Stones, the British rock group that, given its members' roots in the blues ("the devil's music") and their infamous antics, has long been associated with devilishness. The seemingly immortal Azazel taunts Hobbes by having each person it takes over sing the Stones' boastful hit "Time Is on My Side" to him. Azazel's motive is to hasten the fall of civilization, and the film's final shot shows a street jammed with people,

Azazel hiding somewhere in the thronging crowd, as the Stones' "Sympathy for the Devil," with lyrics about Satan's influence on the violence and intolerance in human history, plays on the soundtrack.

CARNIVAL OF SOULS

The various manifestations of departed souls—ghosts, specters, phantoms, spirits, poltergeists—"give a form to the fear of death" (Kawin 111). Yet because at the same time they embody our need to believe in some form of afterlife, the world beyond has often been depicted as being essentially continuous with our own, though perhaps with wispy clouds underfoot. It is reassuring to think that there is life beyond this one and that it is comfortably like our own, merely an extension of it, albeit with winged angels often depicted at filing cabinets following established procedures. In *A Guy Named Joe* (1943), for example, Peter Sandidge (Spencer Tracy) is a reckless bomber pilot who is killed doing a risky maneuver during a mission and in the afterlife is given a new assignment, to accompany and help young pilots in training. Military hierarchy still exists in this afterlife, all the spirit soldiers still wearing their uniforms and saluting each other according to the protocols of rank. Not only did such a vision of the afterlife's familiarity comfort home-front audiences during wartime, when the film was released, but it also further confirmed that God was on our side (we do not see any angels aiding Japanese pilots).

As part of this imagined continuity between this life and the next, supernatural monsters tend to haunt movies because of personal issues for which, like the living, they need closure. As someone explains of all the gathered spirits in *13 Ghosts* (1960), they are "unhappily earthbound because of unsolved problems," unable to move on to the afterlife until justice in some form is served. Often ghosts merely want to do whatever is necessary in order to break the curse that binds them so that then they can at last rest in peace. So, for example, spirits haunt the suburban California home of the Freeling family in *Poltergeist* (1982) because the developer of the housing subdivision of which it is a part had built over a cemetery and had moved only the headstones but left the caskets with the bodies of the deceased. The undead are often trapped by their limbo state and would prefer to rest in peace: as the undead count (Bela Lugosi) wistfully reflects in *Dracula*, "To die, to be *really* dead, that must be glorious."

Before the 1970s, many of the films featuring the supernatural, often in the form of ghosts or spirits, were comedies or romances. This tendency for benevolent ghosts was fueled by the success of the *Topper* films (*Topper* [1937], *Topper Takes a Trip* [1939], *Topper Returns* [1931]), in which a rich and irresponsible married couple, George and Marian Kerby, die in a car crash and come back as ghosts. The *Topper* series was popular enough to generate a television sitcom two decades later that ran for three seasons (1953–55). Comedy duo Abbott and Costello, in addition to meeting classic monsters Frankenstein, the Invisible Man, the Mummy, and Dr. Jekyll and Mr. Hyde, also meet spirits in *Hold That Ghost* (1941) and are themselves ghosts in *The Time of Their Lives* (1946). And later, in the 1960s, when camp became a dominant aesthetic mode, its self-aware humor was anticipated by William Castle's *13 Ghosts*, in which a family inherits a haunted house complete with a spooky housekeeper played by Margaret Hamilton, a cultural icon remembered primarily for her role as the Wicked Witch of the West in *The Wizard of Oz* (1939). Throughout the film, the family wonders whether she is really a witch, and in the film's final shot, Hamilton nods to the camera—and the audience—with a raising of her eyebrows as she picks up a broomstick, although whether to clean house or fly away is left to our imagination.

Romantic ghost movies tend to play on the connection between desire and the supernatural, as when we describe someone we find attractive as "enchanting," "charming," or "spellbinding." *I Married a Witch* (1942), featuring Veronica Lake as the bewitching bride whose love potion comically backfires, plays with this idea. And in *Ghost* (1990), a banker, Sam Wheat (Patrick Swayze), loves his girlfriend, Molly (Demi Moore), so much that his love survives him. Sam is murdered by thieving coworker Carl (Tony Goldwyn) and as a ghost tries to warn Molly that she too is in danger by enlisting the aid of a reluctant medium, Oda Mae Brown (Whoopi Goldberg), who can hear his voice. Sam saves the day, and Carl is killed in the climactic confrontation. Reassuring us that our moral order remains intact, Carl is taken below, while Sam then ascends heavenward. Before this, the worst thing Sam does as a ghost is to keep singing the inane, repetitive pop tune "I'm Henry the Eighth, I Am" until the initially resistant Oda Mae agrees to help him. Instead of being about the ghost as monster, the film emphasizes the loving and sensual connection between Molly and Sam that transcends even death.

Some ghost movies even have ghosts that are entirely benevolent, as in *It's a Wonderful Life* (1946), in which the guardian angel Clarence (Henry Travers), assigned to a troubled family man, George Bailey (Jimmy Stewart), convinces him not to commit suicide because his life is intertwined with that of so many other people. These comical and romantic ghost movies express the reasons for our faith, while the supernatural monster films articulate our fears and doubts. Torn as we are between these conflicting sentiments, our supernatural monsters—vampires, werewolves, mummies, ghosts—are often undead, caught in different ways in a limbo state between life and death.

Supernatural monster movies raise thorny theological questions for us about the existence of God and the reason why things are as they are. *Hellbenders* (2010) treats the knotty issue of God's purpose explicitly in its depiction of the imaginary Augustine Interfaith Order of Hellbound Saints, a team of interdenominational and blasphemous priests who live in New York City in continual debauchery in order to attract demons and then drag them to Hell. Within the film, the characters themselves question the dubious philosophical theology of the Order, but the irony of their approach underscores the theological dilemma raised by all tales of the supernatural, as, in a quite different way, does the French film *Martyrs* (2008), in which a cult of bourgeois people are so desperate for spiritual transcendence that they torture their victims to death in order to achieve it by proxy.

MONSTROUS MACHINATIONS

Just as the zombie has evolved from frighteningly blank and lacking will, as in such earlier movies as *White Zombie* and *I Walked with a Zombie*, to being cannibalistic and quick in films like *28 Days Later . . .* (2002) and *The Girl with All the Gifts* (2016), so in more recent supernatural movies, ghosts and other manifestations of the supernatural have tended to be cruel rather than kind, to cause more death and destruction than mere disturbance. In the early 1970s, with the unpopular war in Vietnam at its height, generating massive and sometimes violent protests across the country (in 1970, unarmed student demonstrators were shot and four killed by the Ohio National Guard at Kent State University) and the Watergate scandal growing (President Richard Nixon resigned in 1974), civil and political institutional order seemed to be crumbling, leading to the cycle of disaster movies, as mentioned in the previous chapter, and to a renaissance of the horror film. *The Exorcist* (1973), released less than a year before Nixon's resignation, is pivotal in this regard: in it, a suddenly unruly adolescent girl, Regan MacNeil (Linda Blair), is possessed by the demon Pazuzu, causing her to commit taboo acts such as stealing, urinating in public, and, perhaps most shocking of all, masturbating with a crucifix. It is no coincidence that Regan lives with her actress mother Chris in Washington, DC, the center of national political power, or that Chris has just completed working on a film about political activism when Regan's problematic behavior begins. To many conservative parents at the time, their rebellious children seemed as if they were possessed. Bob Clark's *Dead of Night* (1974) reverses this idea with its story of a young Vietnam veteran returning home as an unwelcome zombie, a comment on the soldier as an unthinking robot.

More recently, economic pressures have seriously threatened middle-class families like the MacNeils of *The Exorcist*. The decline of the United States' industrial and manufacturing sectors, the great economic recession of 2008, and the widening gap between the rich and poor have challenged the security of average families. The economy is a large and, to many people, intangible and incomprehensible force over which we have no control, like the supernatural. Being pushed over the fiscal cliff, as experts described the growing economic crisis at the time, and falling into the pit of penury is the subject of Sam Raimi's *Drag Me to Hell* (2009). Christine Brown (Alison Lohman) is a loan officer at a branch bank who is competing with her colleague for the vacant job of assistant manager. She wants to move up the corporate ladder, so in order to impress her boss and demonstrate that she has the ruthlessness necessary to succeed in the world of business, Christine puts aside her feelings of sympathy for an old gypsy woman who asks for a further extension on her mortgage and decides to foreclose her loan. Christine is cursed by the old woman, and after being subjected to a series of typical horrors, she is literally pulled by a demon over the "cliff," in this case the edge of a railway platform, and down into the netherworld.

In *Dark Skies* (2013), an average middle-class American family, the Barretts, is targeted by "the Grays," aliens who have been lurking on Earth undetected for some time and experimenting with humans for reasons unknown, analogous to the way the youngest of the two Barrett boys, Sam, keeps a tailless lizard in a box for his amusement. The Barretts wonder why they have been singled out by the Grays but are told by Edwin Pollard (J. K. Simmons), a lone investigator who has been studying them for years, that it has happened to many others and, "there's nothing special about you." The first third of the film, in which the Barretts suddenly find things moved around in their house—lit candles arranged in a geometric fashion in the living room, family photos missing from their frames— push the film, despite its premise involving aliens, into the realm of supernatural horror, especially in the tight closeups of Lacy Barrett (Keri Russell) as she moves through the house at night. The Grays might just as well be poltergeists, and when Lacy's husband, Daniel (Josh Hamilton), sets up a computer monitoring system in his home to investigate the cause of the strange events, the film is clearly referencing the earlier *Paranormal Activity* (2007), which posits a similar situation (along with possession by an evil spirit).

The Barretts' suffering from the tormenting whims of the Grays, which begins when Daniel is laid off and economic pressures begin to mount, could apparently happen to any family. The Grays, says Daniel, make life "a living hell" for them as they become fearful of incursions into the house they are striving so hard to keep. The Barretts try in vain to fight off the Grays, taking such precautions as boarding up all the doors and windows to their house, evoking both Romero's *Night of the Living Dead* and the images of foreclosed homes that were broadcast regularly on television news when the country was deep in the recession. In fact, a similar image is one of the first images we see in the opening establishing montage of the Barretts' middle-class neighborhood. In this sense, *Dark Skies* overlaps with the home-invasion cycle, which unsurprisingly has emerged as a distinct horror subgenre in the new millennium with such films as *Funny Games* (1997; American version 2007), *Panic Room* (2002), *You're Next* (2011), and *The Purge* (2013) and its sequels. All of these films express the fear of vulnerability regarding the integrity of the familial home.

MONSTROUS AMBIGUITY

The possibility that a supernatural occurrence may actually be the result of individual or mass hysteria or—as with other types of monsters already discussed—repression is often treated with narrative ambiguity, declining to disclose an explanation for the film's odd events or withholding them until the end. Such ambiguity has been a common textual strategy of supernatural tales since the rise of Gothic fiction in the late eighteenth century, in which seemingly otherworldly phenomena like rattling chains in the castle, moving suits of armor, and so forth were typically revealed to be the machinations of devious humans rather than the manifestation of devilish spirits. So, for example, in *The Haunting* (1963), it may be that the mysterious and frightening phenomena occurring at Hill House are less the result of paranormal activity than of the repressed guilt and sexual desire of Eleanor (Julie Harris), a member of the investigating team. Similarly, in *The Entity* (1982), an unseen monstrous force haunts Carla Moran (Barbara Hershey) by sexually taunting and titillating her, at one point bringing her to orgasm by massaging her breasts while she is sleeping, and later raping her. While other people eventually witness the attacks, there is the strong suggestion, endorsed by Carla's psychiatrist (Ron Silver), that she has been so sexually traumatized as a child and repressed as an adult that her symptoms have become powerfully haptic, like stigmata.

For Amelia Wilson, the Devil, "as his powers and tactics evolved over the course of Western history, becomes both cause and explanation for the existence of evil, greed, lust, deceit, and general bad behavior. As the personification of sin, he also comes to be associated with all the Commandment-breaking sensual pleasures of human indulgence and desire that Christianity preached against" (14). As for the vampire, Freudian disciple Ernest Jones similarly wrote in his famous essay "On the Nightmare of Bloodsucking," "a nightly visit from a beautiful or frightful being, who first exhausts the sleeper with passionate embraces and then withdraws from him a vital fluid: all this can point only to a natural and common process, namely to nocturnal emissions accompanied with dreams of a more or less erotic nature. In the unconscious mind blood is commonly an equivalent for semen" (119).

Jones was a disciple of Freud, but one does not need Freud to understand the obviously erotic connotations of the vampire as classically represented by Dracula. Universal's publicity tagline for its 1931 film with Bela Lugosi, which launched the vampire film in Hollywood, was, "The strangest love a man has ever known!" and it was released on Valentine's Day 1931. In the film, as in Bram Stoker's source novel, the vampiric count clearly represents an unleashed and frightening sexual energy that was strongly repressed during the Victorian era, when the novel was published. Van Helsing, far from the action-hero makeover he received for the 2004 film *Van Helsing*, is in the novel an avuncular paternal figure of benevolent patriarchy. When he and the young hero, Jonathan Harker, destroy the vampire by tracking him to his lair and impaling him, they effectively limit the libido by channeling desire into the acceptable form of monogamous heterosexuality. In the film's final shot, with Dracula now finally staked and able to rest in peace, the young couple, Jonathan and Mina, ascend a long staircase to the heavenly light of day, accompanied by the promise of wedding bells on the soundtrack as the final fadeout suggests they will live happily ever after. Many vampire films since have played with the sexual implications of the vampire myth.

The characteristic narrative ambiguity of supernatural horror is beautifully exploited in Robert Eggers's *The Witch* (2015), a tale of possible witchcraft and sorcery set in seventeenth-century New England. In Nathaniel Hawthorne's classic short story "Young Goodman Brown" (1835), set during the same period, the young Puritan of the title must leave his wife, the aptly named Faith, and travel through the woods in the dark of night for a reason never stated, although on a metaphorical level, it may be understood as a spiritual journey into the darkness of doubt. "'My love and my Faith,' replied young Goodman Brown, 'of all nights in the year, this one night must I tarry away from thee'" (Hawthorne 149). In the forest, Brown comes upon a fellow who seems to be the Devil and then a witches' coven that apparently includes several respectable citizens of the town. Hawthorne never makes it clear whether Brown experiences a vision or actuality, constantly qualifying his descriptions of events—the stranger's "snake-like staff actually seemed to wriggle in sympathy" (152), for example, or "he seemed to fly along the forest path rather than to walk or run" (157)—and Brown himself is not sure. But the ambiguity has crushed Brown's initial naïve optimism in goodness: "My Faith is gone!" he cries (157), and his fate is to become "a distrustful, if not a desperate man" whose "dying hour was gloom" (163) because he could no longer be certain of distinguishing good and evil again when he looked in the faces of others.

In *The Witch*, William (Ralph Ineson), his wife, Katherine (Kate Dickie), and their children, Thomasin (Anya Taylor-Joy), Caleb (Harvey Scrimshaw), and fraternal twins Mercy and Jonas, are banished from a Puritan community because of their differences over interpreting the New Testament. The family departs into the wilderness and establishes its own farm on the edge of a forest. Katherine soon gives birth to her fifth child, Samuel, who mysteriously vanishes while being watched by Thomasin. We then see that Samuel has been kidnapped by a witch living in the woods, who kills him; but, like all that follows as the family spirals into mutual and fatal recrimination and fear, this scene could be read as literally happening or as the overheated imagination of a devout Christian living in a strange new world and unsure whether events are divine signs of election or damnation. The same might be said about Caleb, who the next day wanders lost in the forest while hunting and comes upon a beautiful and seductive young woman in a hut: the woman may be a witch who enchants Caleb, making him ill and eventually killing him, or his own unbearable guilt at the awakening of adolescent sexuality. The fear of God's displeasure and the possibility of the Devil's influence results in the parents becoming afraid of their own children and boarding them up in the goat stable.

In the film's conclusion, William is gored to death by the family's goat "Black Phillip," and Thomasin in self-defense is forced to kill her mother, who has attacked her in a superstitious frenzy. Then Thomasin speaks to "Black Phillip," who reveals itself as Satan in disguise. He invites her into the forest, where, wandering naked, she discovers a fire-lit coven in the blackness of night like the one Goodman Brown stumbles upon. She joins them, laughingly levitating herself in the dark forest night in the film's eerie final shot. Yet even this event may not actually be happening but instead may be the feverish delusion of a now overwhelmingly guilty and likely insane girl who has just committed matricide.

The key to reading the film's supernatural occurrences as subjective visions is the scene in which Katherine, grieving over her lost baby, seems to have found him and taken him to her breast. She is shown suckling him in close-up; but then the film cuts to a long shot—distanced, hence more objective—showing Katherine with a raven plucking at her breast instead of the baby, and we realize, in retrospect, that the shots of her holding the baby were her imagination. The next morning, as William arises from the conjugal bed, Katherine is briefly seen remaining in bed pretending to be asleep but concealing the blood stains on the front of her white shift. Understanding *The Witch* requires us to read its images carefully, just as Puritans were obsessed with finding God's will in material phenomena.

MONSTROUS MEDIA

In contrast to the narrative ambiguity of many supernatural narratives, there is no question about the fears regarding technology in many of these films, where it usually serves as a portal into another plane of being. Supernatural sounds are heard over baby monitors in *Insidious*. TV functions as a passage into another dimension in *Poltergeist* and into the afterlife in *White Noise* (2005). In David Cronenberg's *Videodrome* (1983), a weaponized video signal causes cancerous tumors and hallucinations in the viewer. Thus infected, television producer Max Renn (James Woods) imagines his adversaries forcibly inserting videotapes that program his behavior into a vagina-like slit that has developed in his abdomen. More recently, the Internet is the site of haunting in *Unfriended* (2014). The film recalls several high-profile cases of teen-agers who committed suicide because of online bullying. In *Unfriended*, which looks like a computer screen of a Skype chat throughout, Laura Berns commits suicide because a humiliating video of her at a party was posted online. A year later, her ghost returns as the uninvited guest "billie227," a literal ghost in the machine seeking brutally fatal revenge on each member of the group.

With the proliferation of social media and "fake news" today, as well as the ability to manipulate digital images in innumerable ways, reality and objective truth have become more difficult to discern. This infernal muddy-ing of the truth status of images informs the contempo-rary cycle of found-footage horror movies. These films feature a variety of monsters—zombies (*Diary of the Dead* [2007], *Quarantine* [2008], a remake of the Span-ish film *[Rec]* [2007]), aliens (*Infection* [2005], *Clover-field* [2008]), and, of course, ghosts and spirits in the *Paranormal Activity* series, *The Last Exorcism* (2009), and *The Devil Inside* (2012)—but they all share a pronounced similarity of style: they unfold in real time, showing footage shot by a camera that is acknowledged by the characters as existing and being present within the narrative world (as opposed to the conventional manner, in which the camera is an invisible observer of events). Often there has been a cataclysmic event of some sort, and the footage is all that remains.

The movie that launched the cycle was *The Blair Witch Project* (1999). Like many of the films that followed in the wake of its success, it explained the film we are watching as found footage made by filmmakers who have disappeared. As the opening titles of *Blair Witch* tell us, "In October of 1994, three student filmmakers disappeared in the woods near Burkittsville, Maryland, while shooting a documentary. A year later, their footage was found." The film that we see is supposedly the footage shot by the three students, chronicling their search for the legendary Blair Witch and their chaotic trip into the woods, where they become lost and terrified and eventually disappear.

Pointing the way for the new-media marketing of films today, the promotional campaign for *The Blair Witch Project* involved the creation of a convincing website with an extremely detailed backstory offering a timeline of events relating to the Blair Witch and the founding of Burkittsville. The website was rich with clickable options for finding out more about the Blair Witch and supposedly historical figures and events. So elaborate was this back-story and website that, as J. P. Telotte has noted, the movie was ancillary to the website, an extension of it. The "project" of *The Blair Witch Project* was the documentary-like creation of the world of the backstory, to which the big-screen film was merely one of the multiple artifacts in its construction. Many people were persuaded that the film was based on historical truth: at the height of its popularity and for some time thereafter, there was a veritable tourist invasion in Burkittsville largely spurred by the convincing details on the website (Robé).

The realist, long-take style of these found-footage monster movies requires digital technology to take shots of such extended length. These monster movies are symptomatic of our postmodern sensibility that, in the digital age, places the truth status of images in doubt. *Cloverfield* explicitly evokes collapsing of the boundaries between documentary and fiction in its evocation of the news coverage of the 9/11 attacks on the World Trade Center in New York City, especially in the scenes that occur during the creature's initial assault. The images in the film of people running through the streets as clouds of dust from buildings destroyed by the monster billow behind, threatening to overtake them, clearly invoke the cell-phone videos taken at ground level during the collapse of the twin towers. The film's advertising image showed a decapitated Statue of Liberty in the foreground, the city's smoking skyline behind—another image strikingly similar to some of the more famous photographic images of 9/11.

In *Cloverfield*, Hud (T. J. Miller) finds a moral mission once he is given the video camera. At first, Hud treats the camera immaturely, using it to voyeuristically film the bodies of attractive women at the party, but as events develop, he embraces his role as a documenter of the monster's attack because, as his friend Rob says, "People are going to want to know how it all went down." Similarly, the amateur filmmakers of *Troll Hunter* (2011) want to expose the national secret of the Troll Security Service because they aspire to be "like Michael Moore." And in *Diary of the Dead*, student filmmaker Jason similarly argues that because he has the equipment, it is his duty to record the truth about the zombie attacks in the absence of the mainstream media and to upload his footage on the Internet so that others might learn how to survive. The monsters of these films generate a need to chronicle them, ghosts in the machine reminding us of the elusive truth of images. As Jean Baudrillard presciently observed, "It is precisely when it appears most truthful, most faithful and most in conformity to reality that the image is most diabolical" (13)—a point that found-footage monster movies have taken literally.

THEM R US

In *The Mist* (2007), directed by Frank Darabont (producer of TV's *The Walking Dead*) from a novella by Stephen King, a group of disparate individuals find themselves trapped by an invasion of otherworldly monsters in a small-town supermarket. The narrative follows illustrator David Drayton (Thomas Jane), who drives into town with his eight-year old son, Billy (Nathan Gamble), for supplies following a violent thunderstorm, along with his neighbor Brent Norton (Andre Braugher). Arriving at the town's supermarket, David notices suspicious police and military activity outside, after which a frantic and injured local man named Dan (Jeffrey DeMunn) runs in warning of danger, in turn followed by a thick fog that quickly envelops the store. After some debate among the people in the market, Norm the bag boy volunteers to go outside, but even before he does, he is snatched away through the shipping-bay door by deadly, unnatural tentacles with rows of articulated fangs as David and some of the others watch in horrified disbelief. When Norm's fate is revealed to all, most of the staff and customers decide to remain inside the market, although some leave, their fates unknown. The market is soon attacked by giant mosquito-like insects as the people try to fend them off with the materials at hand in the store, but some of the creatures gain entry, followed by even larger monsters that look like alien pterodactyls. Some of the people are killed and severely wounded in the fight. On a foray to the adjacent pharmacy for medicine to treat the wounded, David and a few of the others find people cocooned by giant spidery creatures that shoot flesh-burning filaments and whose multitudinous young burst from their human hosts and scatter.

Unable to communicate with the outside world and faced with the unknown and inexplicable, many of the people trapped in the market rally around a religious fanatic, Mrs. Carmody (Marcia Gay Harden), who begins preaching about Judgment Day and a wrathful God. Eventually, she demands that Billy be handed over as a sacrifice to appease the angry Lord. David forms a bond of understanding with Amanda (Laurie Holden), a woman who becomes a surrogate mother for Billy, when the boy goes into shock, and along with her and a few others, they decide to leave. The store's assistant manager, Ollie (Toby Jones), eventually shoots Mrs. Carmody when her faction, which has already sacrificed a soldier to a giant insectoid creature outside, seeks to prevent them from leaving. The group runs through the fog-enshrouded parking lot to David's Land Rover, planning to drive as far away as possible in the hope of escaping the bounds of the unearthly mist.

Only David, Billy, Amanda, Dan, and the town's primary school teacher Irene (Frances Sternhagen) make it to the car. They drive through a haze of destruction, past David's home, where they see his dead wife and cross paths with an enormous creature shrouded in the mist that thunders past. When the car runs out of gas, the group agrees that there is no point in going on and make a final pact: David has enough bullets in Amanda's gun to shoot all of them except himself. Steeling himself to the monstrous task, David proceeds to shoot each of them in the head, including his son, who awakes just in time to register horror on his face as it dawns on him that his father, who has assured him throughout that he will keep him safe, is about to kill him.

The film cuts from Billy's horrified expression to a long shot of the car, sparing us the graphic sight of the boy's death, but even through the shrouding mist, we can see a flash of gunfire briefly light up the vehicle's interior with each bullet. Afterward, David exits the car in anguish, waiting to be killed by one of the creatures of the mist. As he waits, an ominous, barely audible clanking sound grows louder, becomes recognizable as mechanical, and is followed by the dim headlights of what becomes discernible as the advancing armored vehicles of the U.S. Army through the now-receding mist. David collapses and screams in anguish as the film ends.

This unremittingly bleak ending, in which the military slowly appears, at first ambiguously, harks back to the conclusion of Ray Milland's earlier *Panic in Year Zero!* (1962), which focuses on the attempt by one family, the Baldwins, to escape the Los Angeles area after it is hit with a nuclear bomb. In the climax of that film, the Baldwins are stopped on the highway by murky headlights, which they, and the viewer, at first assume to be from the cars of the hot-rodding youths who earlier were taunting them; but it turns out to be the military, and the film ends happily rather than horribly with the family rescued rather than ravaged. Never mind that one of the nation's major cities has been obliterated, *Panic in Year Zero!*'s comfortable closure suggests that despite such an enormous catastrophe, order can and will be restored by government. In *The Mist*, by contrast, the arrival of the military signals a hollow victory, because David Drayton is left with the consequences of his monstrous actions, his family and friends all dead at his hand. All traditional verities have failed: science and the military are viewed with suspicion, as are one's neighbors; and the character we are led to believe throughout is the conventional male hero, protector of women and children, has become a death-wielding monster.

The film's monsters are many and varied, and they lurk everywhere, in plain sight as well as out there in the mist. They are the monstrous embodiment of the various repressed angers and fears of the characters, a catalogue of several discussed in this book. A cross-section of Americans with regard to race, gender, and class, the film's characters all go about their daily business alongside one another until the moment of monstrous crisis happens, and then their angers come to the fore and they turn on each other. Norton, a black man, makes a fatal decision to leave the market in part because of his wariness of the townsfolk, a white community of which he already feels himself an outsider. Class conflict, too, quickly arises when Jim (William Sadler), a repairman in overalls and work cap who resents the wealthier customers whose appliances he services, overreacts to David when David contradicts him and urges Norm not to go outside. And religious fundamentalism flares into fanaticism, separating the people into two hostile groups, which broadly mirrors the ideological divide of the nation today and which soon leads to bloodshed. Ironically, these bloody tensions between the characters take place in a supermarket, among the shelves and rows of ample consumer goods, including household items that can be used to fight off monsters, suggesting that these conflicts and animosities are microcosmic of the nation, the American Dream turned to nightmare.

Although released more than a decade ago, *The Mist* nevertheless seems especially relevant now when the nation in the Trump era is more divided than since the 1960s and when violence regularly threatens to replace reasoned debate. It remains to be seen what movie monsters will come to characterize the period, what horrifying creatures popular culture will find more apposite to the age than the zombie, which has been the monster of the passing millennial moment. For Ian Olney, the zombie has been so popular because it is able to reflect such cultural anxieties as terrorism, contemporary alienation, social and economic collapse, and infectious diseases and global pandemics at the same time as it allows for a premise that functions as "a kind of cultural wish fulfillment, catering to current fantasies about life in a postapocalyptic world without social structures or laws, where survival is paramount and violence is not simply permitted but necessary and justified" (8).

Olney goes on to suggest that the zombie has become so pervasive in popular culture because, sadly, we recognize our kinship with the undead. This may be so, but *The Mist* shows us with all the power of which monster cinema is capable that, whatever horrifying creatures we might call forth from the obscure regions of our imagination, whether human, natural, or supernatural, they are our monsters; and our very survival depends on that recognition.

ACKNOWLEDGMENTS

I am indebted to Leslie Mitchener, editor in chief and associate director at Rutgers University Press, for our engaging conversations and her unwavering support, which led to the genesis of this book. Many thanks, too, to Quick Takes series editors Gwendolyn Audrey Foster and Wheeler Winston Dixon for developing this exciting series concept and for their enthusiastic appreciation of my work. Andrew Katz was a wonderfully attentive copyeditor.

Research by Kevin McGuiness, a doctoral student in the Interdisciplinary Ph.D. in the Humanities Program at Brock University, Ontario, Canada, helped shape some of my thinking about monster culture. Thanks also to Rob Latham, Christopher Sharrett, Dan Barnowski, and Denis Dyack, all of whom have helped in ways known and unknown.

FURTHER READING

Asma, Stephen. *On Monsters: An Unnatural History of Our Worst Fears*. New York: Oxford UP, 2011.

Carroll, Noël. *The Philosophy of Horror, or, Paradoxes of the Heart*. New York: Routledge, 1990.

Clarens, Carlos. *An Illustrated History of the Horror Film*. New York: Capricorn, 1967.

Clover, Carol J. *Men, Women, and Chain Saws: Gender in the Modern Horror Film*. Princeton, NJ: Princeton UP, 1992.

Creed, Barbara. *The Monstrous-Feminine: Film, Feminism, Psychoanalysis*. New York: Routledge, 1993.

Gifford, Denis. *Movie Monsters*. New York: Dutton, 1969.

Grant, Barry Keith, ed. *The Dread of Difference: Gender and the Horror Film*. 2nd ed. Austin: U of Texas P, 2015.

Grant, Barry Keith, and Christopher Sharrett, eds. *Planks of Reason: Essays on the Horror Film*. Rev. ed. Lanham, MD: Scarecrow, 2004.

Hendershot, Cyndy. *I Was a Cold War Monster: Horror Films, Eroticism and the Cold War Imagination*. Bowling Green, OH: Popular Press, 2001.

Huss, Roy, and T. J. Ross, eds. *Focus on the Horror Film*. Englewood Cliffs, NJ: Prentice-Hall, 1972.

Jancovich, Mark. *Rational Fears: American Horror in the 1950s*. Manchester: Manchester UP, 2006.

Kawin, Bruce. *Horror and the Horror Film*. New York: Anthem, 2012.

King, Stephen. *Danse Macabre*. New York: Everest House, 1981.

Landis, Jon. *Monsters in the Movies*. London: Dorling Kindersley, 2016.

Skal, David J. *The Monster Show: A Cultural History of Horror*. New York: Norton, 1994.

Sobchack, Vivian. *Screening Space: The American Science Fiction Film*. 2nd enlarged ed. New Brunswick, NJ: Rutgers UP, 2004

Tudor, Andrew. *Monsters and Mad Scientists: A Cultural History of the Horror Movie*. London: Basil Blackwell, 1989.

Waller, Gregory, ed. *American Horrors: Essays on the Modern Horror Film*. Urbana: U of Illinois P, 1987.

———. *The Living and the Undead: From Stoker's "Dracula" to Romero's "Dawn of the Dead."* Urbana: U of Illinois P, 1986.

Wells, Paul. *The Horror Genre: From Beelzebub to Blair Witch*. London: Wallflower, 2000.

Wood, Robin, and Richard Lippe, eds. *The American Nightmare: Essays on the Horror Film*. Toronto: Festival of Festivals, 1979.

WORKS CITED

Asma, Stephen. *On Monsters: An Unnatural History of Our Worst Fears*. New York: Oxford UP, 2011.

Baudrillard, Jean. *The Evil Demon of Images*. Sydney: Power Institute of Fine Arts, U of Sydney, 1987.

Baxter, John. *Science Fiction in the Cinema*. New York: Paperback Library, 1970.

Beard, William, and Piers Handling. "The Interview." *The Shape of Rage: The Films of David Cronenberg*. Ed. Piers Handling. Toronto: Academy of Canadian Cinema, 1983. 159–98.

Biskind, Peter. *Seeing Is Believing: How Hollywood Taught Us to Stop Worrying and Love the Fifties*. New York: Pantheon, 1982.

Brottman, Mikita. "Ritual, Tension and Relief: The Terror of *The Tinger*." *Planks of Reason: Essays on the Horror Film*. Rev. ed. Ed. Barry Keith Grant and Christopher Sharrett. Lanham, MD: Scarecrow, 2004. 265–82.

Butler, Ivan. *Horror in the Cinema*. New York: A. S. Barnes, 1970.

Carroll, Noël. *The Philosophy of Horror, or, Paradoxes of the Heart*. New York: Routledge, 1990.

Carson, Rachel. *Silent Spring*. New York: Houghton Mifflin, 1962.

Clover, Carol J. *Men, Women, and Chain Saws: Gender in the Modern Horror Film*. Princeton, NJ: Princeton UP, 1992.

Dika, Vera. "The Stalker Film, 1978–81." *American Horrors: Essays on the Modern Horror Film*. Ed. Gregory A. Waller. Urbana: U of Illinois P, 1987. 86–101.

Dillard, R. H. W. *Horror Films*. New York: Monarch, 1976.

Douglas, Drake. *Horror!* New York: Collier, 1969.

Evans, Walter. "Monster Movies: A Sexual Theory." *Planks of Reason: Essays on the Horror Film*. Ed. Barry Keith Grant. Lanham, MD: Scarecrow, 1996. 53–64.

Freud, Sigmund. *New Introductory Lectures on Psychoanalysis*. Ed. and trans. James Strachey. New York: Norton, 1964.

Gettings, Fred. *Ghosts in Photographs: The Extraordinary Story of Spirit Photography*. New York: Harmony Books, 1978.

Gifford, Denis. *Movie Monsters*. New York: Dutton, 1969.

Greenberg, Harvey J. *The Movies on Your Mind: Film Classics on the Couch from Fellini to Frankenstein*. New York: Saturday Review Press / Dutton, 1975.

Hammond, Paul. *Marvelous Méliès*. London: Gordon Fraser, 1974.

Hark, Ina Rae. "Crazy Like a Prof.: Mad Science and the Transgression of the Rational." *Bad: Infamy, Darkness, Evil, and Slime on Screen*. Ed. Murray Pomerance. Albany: State U of New York P, 2004. 301–14.

Hawkins, Joan. "'One of Us': Tod Browning's *Freaks*." *Freakery: Cultural Spectacles of the Extraordinary Body*. Ed. Rosemary Garland Thomson. New York: NYU P, 1996. 265–76.

Hawthorne, Nathaniel. *Selected Tales and Sketches*. 3rd ed. Ed. Hyatt H. Waggoner. New York: Holt, Rinehart and Winston, 1970.

Heimer, Mel. *The Cannibal: The Case of Albert Fish*. Secaucus, NJ: Lyle Stuart, 1971.

Hitchcock, Alfred. "On Style: An Interview with *Cinema*." *Hitchcock on Hitchcock: Selected Writings and Interviews*. Ed. Sidney Gottlieb. Berkeley: University of California Press, 1995. 285–302.

Huss, Roy, and T. J. Ross, eds. *Focus on the Horror Film*. Englewood Cliffs, NJ: Prentice-Hall, 1972.

Jones, Ernest. *On the Nightmare*. London: Hogarth, 1931.

Kawin, Bruce. "Children of the Light." *Film Genre Reader IV*. Ed. Barry Keith Grant. Austin: U of Texas P, 2012. 360–81.

———. *Horror and the Horror Film*. New York: Anthem, 2012.

Kearney, Richard. *Strangers, Gods, and Monsters: Interpreting Otherness*. New York: Routledge, 2002.

King, Stephen. *Danse Macabre*. New York: Everest House, 1981.

Kracauer, Siegfried. *From Caligari to Hitler: A Psychological History of the German Film*. Princeton, NJ: Princeton UP, 1947.

Kristeva, Julia. *Powers of Horror: An Essay on Abjection*. Trans. Leon S. Roudiez. New York: Columbia UP, 1982.

McNally, Raymond, and Radu Florescu. *In Search of Dracula*. New York: Warner Paperback Library, 1973.

Olney, Ian. *Zombie Cinema*. New Brunswick, NJ: Rutgers UP, 2017.

Pine, Joslyn, ed. *The Book of African American Quotations*. Mineola, NY: Dover, 2011.

Robé, Christopher. "In Search of Burkittsville." *Nothing That Is: Millennial Cinema and the Blair Witch Controversies*. Ed. Sarah L. Higley and Jeffrey Andrew Weinstock. Detroit: Wayne State UP, 2004. 217–28.

Ruddick, Nicholas. *Science Fiction Adapted to Film*. Canterbury, UK: Gylphi, 2016.

Skal, David J. *The Monster Show: A Cultural History of Horror*. New York: Norton, 1994.

Sobchack, Thomas. "Genre Film: A Classical Experience." *Film Genre Reader IV*. Ed. Barry Keith Grant. Austin: U of Texas P, 2012. 121–32.

Sobchack, Vivian. *Screening Space: The American Science Fiction Film*. 2nd enlarged ed. New Brunswick, NJ: Rutgers UP, 2004

Sontag, Susan. "The Aesthetics of Destruction." *Against Interpretation and Other Essays*. New York: Delta, 1966. 209–25.

Telotte, J. P. "*The Blair Witch Project* Project: Film and the Internet." *Nothing That Is: Millennial Cinema and the Blair Witch Controversies*. Ed. Sarah L. Higley and Jeffrey Andrew Weinstock. Detroit: Wayne State UP, 2004. 37–51.

Tudor, Andrew. *Monsters and Mad Scientists: A Cultural History of the Horror Movie*. London: Basil Blackwell, 1989.

Wandrei, Donald A. "Something from Above." *Weird Tales* Dec. 1930: 763–78.

Wells, H. G. Preface. *Seven Famous Novels by H. G. Wells*. New York: Knopf, 1934. vii–x.

Williams, Linda. "Film Bodies: Gender, Genre, and Excess."
Film Genre Reader IV. Ed. Barry Keith Grant. Austin:
U of Texas P, 2012. 159–77.

———. "When the Woman Looks." *The Dread of Difference:
Gender and the Horror Film*. 2nd ed. Ed. Barry Keith
Grant. Austin: U of Texas P, 2015. 17–36.

Williams, Linda Ruth. *The Erotic Thriller in Contemporary
Cinema*. Bloomington: Indiana UP, 2005.

Wilson, Amelia. *The Devil*. London: Barron's, 2002.

Wolf, Leonard. *Monsters*. San Francisco: Straight Arrow
Books, 1974.

Wood, Robin. "Beauty Bests the Beast." *American Film* 8.10
(Sept. 1983): 63–65.

———. "Gods and Monsters." *Film Comment* 14.5 (Sept.–
Oct. 1978): 19–25.

———. *Hitchcock's Films Revisited*. New York: Columbia
UP, 1989.

———. "An Introduction to the American Horror Film."
The American Nightmare: Essays on the Horror Film. Ed.
Robin Wood and Richard Lippe. Toronto: Toronto:
Festival of Festivals, 1979. 7–28.

INDEX

ABOUT THE AUTHOR

Barry Keith Grant is Emeritus Professor of Film Studies and Popular Culture at Brock University in Ontario, Canada. He is the author or editor of many books, including *Planks of Reason: Essays on the Horror Film, The Dread of Difference: Gender and the Horror Film,* and *Invasion of the Body Snatchers.* An Elected Fellow of the Royal Society of Canada, Grant's writing has appeared in numerous journals and anthologies.